The CoachCompass®

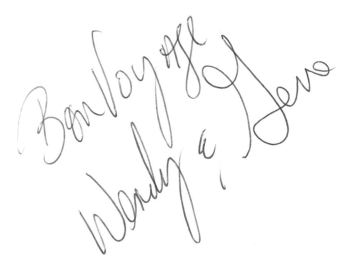

The **CoachCompass®**

Navigation Tools for Career and Life Success

Wendy B. Adams

Gene A. Pometto, Jr.

iUniverse, Inc.
New York Lincoln Shanghai

The **CoachCompass**®
Navigation Tools for Career and Life Success

iUniverse books may be ordered through booksellers or by contacting:

iUniverse
2021 Pine Lake Road, Suite 100
Lincoln, NE 68512
www.iuniverse.com
1-800-Authors (1-800-288-4677)

ISBN-13: 978-0-595-34528-1 (pbk)
ISBN-13: 978-0-595-79278-8 (ebk)
ISBN-10: 0-595-34528-X (pbk)
ISBN-10: 0-595-79278-2 (ebk)

Printed in the United States of America

This book is lovingly dedicated to the memory of our dear friend, Duane Charlow. Duane reminds us of our universal birthright to first define our success, and then experience that success wherever we are and with whatever we choose to do or be!

CONTENTS

ACKNOWLEDGMENTS

There are so many people who contributed to the final publication of this book. Space limitations preclude listing them all; however, we offer special thanks to:

Our friends and colleagues, Joan and Marvin Adams, and Mick Magill, for listening to our early ideas and encouraging us to move forward;

Our friend and colleague, Shala Pulgar, whose infectious enthusiasm and vision provided a clearer focus and direction;

Our friend and colleague, Jessica Malone, for creating the first visual rendering of the **CoachCompass®**;

Our friends, Jan and Eric Willison from JanEric Arts, for the wonderful back cover portrait.

Author and friend, Wendy Enelow, for her initial interest in this project and for the opportunity to promote these ideas within the coaching community;

Special thanks to graphic designer Courtney Block of Block Design in Baltimore. Without her skill, talent, and responsiveness, we would have floated out to sea;

We also extend our heartfelt gratitude to our families, without whom we would not be the people that we are today;

Finally, to the people who told us (sometimes more than once) that everyone, indeed *anyone*, could use this information. We are eternally in your debt.

FOREWORD

Charting Your Career Course

When you think of success in your career and your life, what comes to mind? Riches, fame, recognition? An adventurous lifelong journey that you will enjoy? Well, the good news is...you get to choose!

Think of your career as a ship that you have selected and equipped; one that you could sail anywhere and everywhere you wished. Of course, this ship should also be prepared for *difficult waters* and *challenging winds*. Early in your life, you were probably introduced to many different "career ships," some dinghies, some yachts. Whatever their size or shape, perhaps a certain course became apparent to you, or maybe you had no particular destination as you embarked on your career journey.

Most assuredly, in addition to influencing your choice of career ship and destination, your parents, teachers, and peers played a tremendous role in coaching you to maintain a solid course toward "familiar waters and known lands." Perhaps you listened to others; perhaps you didn't. Now, for whatever reasons, you may feel as though you need a new direction-finder for your career.

To achieve the full potential of your career course, you must first chart it. This book will help you do that. Here you will find the tools to review and examine it in detail. This may be the first time you have ever attempted such an exercise. Just remember, your goal is to identify those things you will need to learn to achieve the level of personal and professional success you deserve.

Over the past 50 years there has been a dramatic change in the career. Historically, work and family life were simple—to a large degree, linear. There were distinct, and often proscribed, starting and ending points. In short, a person entered "here" and exited "there." Unless one chose an unusual vocational path, certain milestones were almost inevitable. Most likely a career was initiated while in youth, progressed into a specific job course, and in the natural course of events, concluded with an inactive retirement.

Today, a career is a never-ending journey that may introduce you to many *ports* and subject you to more than a few *storms*. Your career may change course several times in a single lifetime. In fact, there may no longer be a final destination we once knew as **retirement.** Rather, your career may spin itself out as a series of unexpected life changes. Thus it is important to be aware that when charting your course for career success (or when helping someone else to chart theirs), a career is a continuous cycle. Viewing your career as a continuous cycle also allows you to identify all of its successful moments and serves in guiding your progress forward, overcoming obstacles as they arise.

The **CoachCompass**® is designed to expand your knowledge of your career and yourself. It is so named because the system provides the expert guidance of a career coach coupled with specific direction-finding tools that you can use to identify your present career location and consequently experience the ideal journey. It is our hope that this information will allow you to navigate this world of work and life with greater ease.

In the beginning, there was only you and the journey...

How successful do you want to be? We have asked this of many clients over the years. Some were not sure what we meant. Others realized that once they defined what *their* success meant, getting there was far more involved than that to which they were willing to commit. Others, who were dedicated to the process, made their career journey a success every step of the way.

Success, by the way, is a self-determined state. It can be as simple or as complex as you wish to make it. Your definition of success may be very different from ours. For everyone, success is always a choice. It is not necessarily wealth, status or accumulation. Success is feeling good about your life, your work, and your family. Only you can decide where life should take you; only you can decide what your success *ship* looks like and where it goes. Along the way, you may experience difficulties as well as some luck. Help and guidance to maneuver through *rough waters* may come in the form of a friend, a counselor, a parent or a coach. The most important trait for this guide is that this person understands what "success" means to you. If this is not the case, it is likely that they will be priming you to *sail* **their** career ship and not your own.

You initially chose the direction your career and life would take when you were very young. In the mode of early self-discovery, as you were developing your self-esteem, gaining independence, and charting your course, external forces began to challenge your impressions and ideas about your self-identity. The question to ask yourself now is, "Do you recognize who you are today within the context of your career and your life?"

To identify the specific requirements for your present career life, consider returning to the source of your journey. Once you define the stages of progression, you will have the potential to overcome any personal and professional obstacles by building upon each experience. In so doing, you will gain a complete view of all that is required to achieve greater happiness and satisfaction in your life.

As always, we wish you the best for your career success!

Wendy & Gene

Introduction: What Was Then Is Now

Gene Speaks:

If you can capture and retain the essence of the person you are from the beginning of your dreams, developing your skills and choices with this authentic self in mind, then it may be possible for you to sustain achievement and experience happiness throughout your entire life.

Thanks to a brilliant woman, Rivalee Gitomer, Wendy was introduced to a truly enlightening learning experience. Rivalee taught Early Childhood Education at the local community college. Personally, we believe she was hiding her genius in all the *right* places. A remarkable teacher, Rivalee knew who she was and how to help others in their self-discovery. Through behavioral observation and creative alternatives to the normal teaching model, Rivalee incorporated methods that were far beyond the lecture approach of the day. We believe that by remaining in a small environment, her greatest gifts to her students were more valued; her personal impact made more substantial.

Rivalee was the quintessential big fish in a little pond. Her primary focus was to help blossoming early childhood education teachers to become effective guides and caretakers for young children. Recognizing that the learning time was short and the demands of the curriculum steep, Rivalee gave class participants numerous and repeated opportunities to observe behavior before she prompted them to draw conclusions, make assumptions or judgments about children. One particular class assignment required that they observe a four-year-old kindergarten child over the period of the entire semester. Wendy was forty-years-old at the time. Before this challenge, she had not given much thought to the career potential of a four-year-old child.

Rivalee required that each class participant observe and document their selected child's activities. This exercise entailed writing observational statements such as: "She put all of the balls into a pile, and then she shoved the balls. As she shoved the balls, she watched them move. As she watched them move, she watched the others watching her." Each student recorded hundreds of observations on their assigned child.

At the end of the semester, after reading and commenting on all of the documented observations, Rivalee requested a final summary statement of what had been witnessed. In Wendy's experience, an observer's judgment appeared to be far less important than their recognizing how authentic the child was being in his/her actions. In reviewing the observations, she realized which activities made the child feel satisfied and successful. Several "aha" moments are recalled here. At the age of four:

- We do what we like because we have discovered that it satisfies us.
- We do what we like because we can *feel* successful at it.
- We will continue to do what we like if we can find value or reward in the activity.
- In the absence of programmed opinions and restrictions, we have unlimited choices.
- We believe that we can do almost anything!

Wendy and I have made similar observations about adults moving through career and life transitions; some of their own making; some imposed by external forces. Here are several of our observations. In career maturity:

- We rarely celebrate our natural talents within our work.
- We often do what we do because we are obligated to do it.
- We watch the 20-, 30- or 40-year *retirement* clock.
- We believe that we have only a few career choices.
- We impose unnecessary limitations on our lives and, therefore, limitations on our success.

What happened to our views between childhood and adulthood? Is it possible to discover at a later stage in life what you were meant to do, finally fulfilling those hidden dreams? We believe so. Here are some additional conclusions based on our combined experience as coaches, counselors, and trainers:

- Recognition of your authentic self at an early age is an important awareness if you are to chart the most appropriate career/life direction. If this self-recognition is not realized and honored, then the actions required for moving you toward an ideal vocational journey may be overlooked. However, it is *never* too late to recognize and choose the authentic you!

- The more that you do what you like early in your life, developing to your strengths in that area throughout your life, the higher the likelihood that you will be happy and successful in what you (eventually) choose to do in your career at *any* age.

- You can effectively plan, develop, manage, and transition within the course of your career *only* if you possess the specific competencies required to overcome any obstacles discovered as you move through the four distinct stages.

- A new beginning can occur at any point within your life. This may happen as a result of your elective choices or external changes beyond your control. You can re-create yourself, your career and your life at any time.

- With the right attitude and knowledge, success is possible for anyone!

Discovering Your Present Location:
A Quick Career Diagnostic

Whenever you are contemplating your career, first consider your starting point. Identifying this starting point will permit you to plan an effective course of action while anticipating any obstacles that may get in your way.

Below are three strategies that will help you to identify your present *location*. These strategies act as recurring themes throughout this book. In your career journey, you will travel step-by-step through the four stages of the Career Lifecycle and the 12 Positions of Career Success; these are the navigational tools of the **CoachCompass®**.

Strategy #1: Define you! On a piece of paper, answer this question: **Who am I?**

> If you found that question difficult to answer, consider how capable you are of representing yourself well to individuals who may hire, promote, or support you in your endeavors!
>
> Take an honest look at yourself. This is not something that we tend to do often. If you are not clear about *who* you are, other people may also find it difficult to pinpoint your identity in terms of work relationships and needs. This identification extends to your personal presentation. How do you package yourself? Are you formal in your dress? Casual? Trendy? Your personal presentation provides clues about how you see yourself and how you wish others to see you. Sometimes changing your approach can positively enrich the direction you are taking.

Strategy #2: Assess you! **What do you do?**

> **Note:** This is not about job titles. For example, if you were to ask us to describe what we do, we would say: "We are **mirrors** for our

clients; we provide them feedback. We are **excavators**; revealing their genuine personal and professional value. We are **guides**; directing them in making sound and appropriate decisions. We are **cheerleaders**; supporting them in all of their choices; motivating them past their defeats and cheering them on through the end of the game."

This second strategy involves identifying the tangible contribution that you bring to your work. What skills and abilities permit measurable outcomes? How are these tangibles conveyed to others in ways that illustrate value within the workplace? Remember, this is about *more* than getting a degree, gaining a certification or holding a job title. What impact do your unique talents have upon the workplace?

Strategy #3: Validate you! **What do you want?**

Ask your family, friends, and coworkers; any of the people with whom you spend time. What drives you to action? What motivates you? How do you celebrate yourself in your actions?

Our third strategy involves your interests as you strive to get what you want from your career. Motivations can vary from tangible things such as money and wealth to non-tangible things such as recognition and respect. Whatever you choose, it is important to determine what truly rewards you the most. What compels or drives you to do what you do?

These three quick strategies should get you thinking about what you have to offer to your own career, and what your career currently offers you. So as you begin, your check-up starts with introspection. Refer to the Appendix to take your own personal **Career Success Check-up.**

Setting Sail

The 12 Positions of Career Success:
Your Career Lifecycle

Before you set sail, you will need to become familiar with the 12
Positions of Career Success, found within the four stages of your **Career
Lifecycle**. The Career Lifecycle is a 360 degree visual template that
provides you with a complete and current map of the four career stages.
It can define your specific needs anywhere along the journey. This
dynamic cycle requires you to plan, develop, manage, and transition
your career effectively by learning both the necessary skills and the
discretionary skills that support you as the cycle of change continues.
The Career Lifecycle is simply a theoretical career/life blueprint. As you
progress through each of the 12 positions and discover the degrees of
learning presented, note the specific strategies, activities, and suggestions compiled for each profile. There are also additional supports and
worksheets in the Appendix. These tools will serve to direct you when
you are feeling stuck, unsuccessful or just plain bored in your career.

Remember, your position will change and shift as you are continuously
affected by new learning, choices, and any external changes in your
personal and professional environment. Identify a good career coach to
help you; to provide support and positive feedback along the way, if you
find the obstacles too difficult.

Review the Career Lifecycle with the four stages to see how the journey
unfolds.

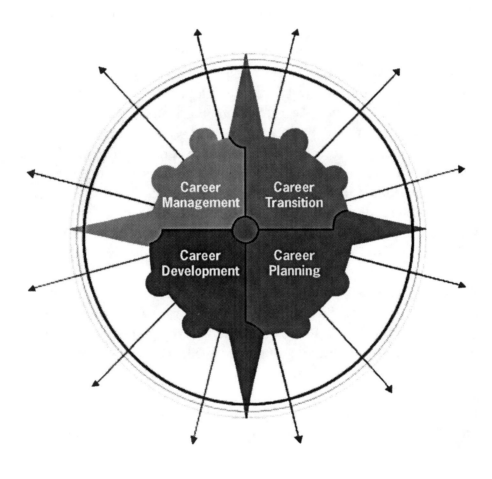

The Career Lifecycle and You

Whenever you chart a career course, you will be required to identify the necessary tools essential for navigating it. The most important tools are those that you can learn to consistently utilize as your career grows and changes. The Career Lifecycle, as your personal mapping tool, provides an easy visual context for your career.

As you view the graphic, starting in the east and moving below the curve to the west, the first six positions of your career, as found along the Career Lifecycle, create the **foundation positions.** Progressing through these various degrees of learning, this *linear* initial **progression** prepares you to navigate the world of work by providing you with the necessary pre-work, planning and development skills that you will *absolutely* require for correctly mapping your career course.

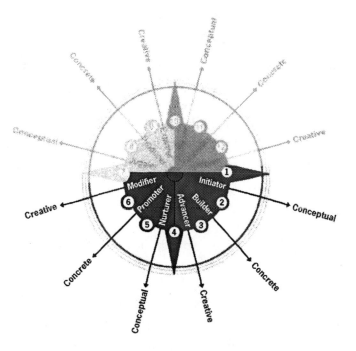

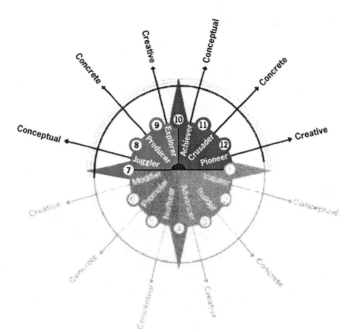

Progressing from the west above the curve back to the east are the *random* potential degrees of learning that you *may* require when you apply your vocational efforts to the workplace or mature in your career. These are the **fluid positions** that hold potential for creating **change** in life. Your ability to continuously learn and apply your skills throughout your Career Lifecycle will allow you to be more effective as you manage and transition your career. Simply presented, if you are able to build and secure a strong foundation through good career planning and development in the first two stages, you will also have an easier time navigating through the changes and challenges when you are managing and transitioning it.

To get a better feel for your personal Career Lifecycle and the entire **CoachCompass**® system, you will have the opportunity to follow a case study of a man named "Will." You will follow him throughout the early benchmarks of his vocational journey to his present successful status in the workplace. Along the way you will be introduced to the events that shaped Will's early career life and learn how he responded to those events.

Will

At the age of four, Will began to show a great interest in animals. It was clear that this curiosity was more than just an enjoyment of pets. His parents and other family members also noticed his compassion for animals.

Fascinated by the work of a family friend, Will would spend hours helping out at the veterinary hospital. Even the most unpleasant of tasks were a delight as he was introduced to a variety of different animals and their unique needs. His parents supported his educational requirement, and encouraged him to develop strong math and science skills. During a particularly difficult course of study, they posted tutorials on the walls of the kitchen and his bedroom to provide visual cues. They enrolled him in summer camps where he could learn more about nature and animals. They also researched scholarship programs and veterinary schools.

Will had to move frequently to acquire his undergraduate, graduate, doctorate degrees and to complete his required internships. The competition for entrance to veterinary school was intense. These obstacles might have deterred others, but this was a lifelong dream for Will; he was determined to make it a reality. Beginning years earlier, he had envisioned himself as "a doctor for animals." Although he had to take various unrelated jobs along the way, each experience provided him with another concrete skill that would strengthen his knowledge base with people, and also contribute to his ability to make better decisions as a doctor.

Today Will is a respected partner in a well-known veterinary practice. As happy and committed today as he was throughout most of his career journey; it would be difficult for you to imagine him doing anything else. His patients and their owners, you can be sure, feel the same way.

Will's ultimate accomplishment is the result of effective vocational planning and development. Choices made through difficult times always aligned his actions with his dreams, permitting him to overcome roadblocks in his path. Will was also fortunate to have identified his goal early in life and to have supportive parents that encouraged him to develop to his interests and strengths.

The "Will" in you deserves to be realized.

The Journey through the Career Lifecycle

Your journey through the Career Lifecycle begins with **Career Planning**. There have been drastic changes in Career Planning since the beginning of the 20th century. In fact, for centuries prior, there was little need to plan a career. The die was cast early, dependent in large part on your cultural background, gender and social class. With few choices available, women and the lower uneducated classes were unlikely to plan their futures.

Over the last hundred years, society has changed the way that we consider and access education; also, how a career is chosen, developed and managed. As a result, it is critically important for you to first identify a general career direction, prior to spending the expensive educational dollar. Considering that most college degrees are rarely applied to gaining or continuing employment in the initial educational discipline, this trend presents a good argument for getting a basic college education, starting a job, and through the work, further defining your specific focus for any additional education pursued.

As you journey through early stages of the Career Lifecycle (especially through the first three degrees of career learning), note that the emphasis centers exclusively on you: your preferences, your capabilities, your interests. Once these have been defined, it will be far easier to navigate through the balance of the learning required.

Are you ready to take on the challenges of charting your career course?

CHAPTER ONE

Stage One of the Career Lifecycle

Your Career Plan

Career Planning: the planning, acquisition and expansion of life and career skills.

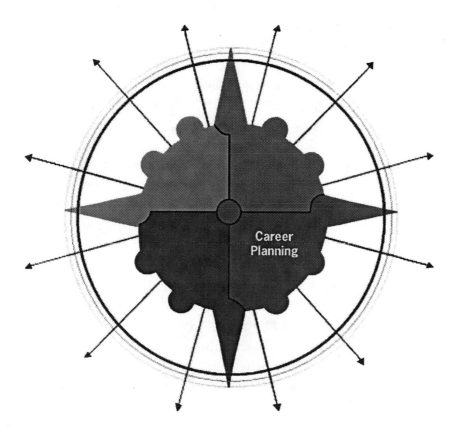

Career Planning is the first and most critical stage. The learning that occurs in this stage relates to, "What I want to do when I grow up." This stage suggests that if you have taken all the correct steps to plan your career well, it is highly likely that you will also be able to manage your career well.

Career Planning, as it begins your personal Career Lifecycle, permits you to clearly define yourself through your preferences, skill predispositions, and innate talents. As you continue to learn about yourself and obtain both preferred and relevant vocational skills, you become better prepared to effectively plan the most appropriate direction.

Career Planning is comprised of three distinct positions or degrees of learning. These correlate to your personal identity, the tangible and innate vocational skills that you possess and may need to develop, and how you will choose to apply these skills toward an identified career direction. These degrees of learning are referred to as positions. Occupying any one of the 12 positions found on the Career Lifecycle means you have the opportunity to either **acquire** the knowledge required of the position or to **apply** your knowledge as you occupy the specific position.

It is possible that you can land in this first position or any of the other 12 positions at any time, or many times as both your personal and professional cycles shift. Your measure of success is determined by how well you meet the demands of this position as it changes over the entire course of your career.

You can liken this example to playing a Monopoly game. Each time you land in a different position on the board, you have things to learn and to consider; also choices to make that will direct your actions. Once you land in the same position several times, you eventually learn the requirements of that position; what you must do, should do or could do while you are there in order to "win" the game!

The first degree of learning in the first stage of Career Planning is called the **Initiator** position. As an Initiator, you are prompted to identify your personal preferences independently from the opinions of others, and take personal initiative for action. Once you learn to make independent life and career decisions, it is likely that you will feel more empowered to make appropriate choices throughout your career whenever you land in this position.

Note: You will see that the **Initiator** is located to the east in the first quadrant of Career Planning.

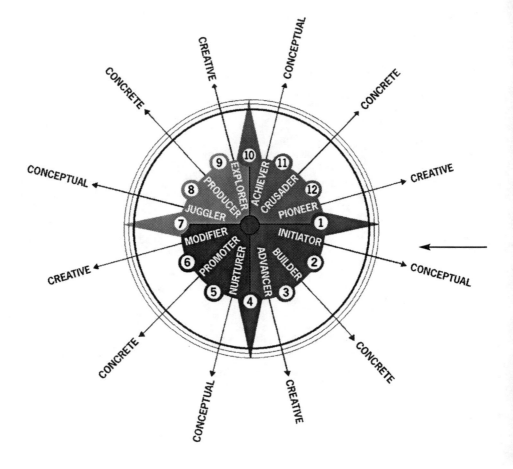

The First Degree of Learning: Who I Am

The Initiator

If you think it is easy to know yourself and to be true to your authentic self, take time to count how often within a 24-hour period you compromise your individuality and desires. In your career planning stage, the Initiator represents the independent, unique and wonderful you! The Initiator is a CONCEPTUAL position defining your self-identity. This view is based on your core expression or self-definition. Why CONCEPTUAL? Primarily, all CONCEPTUAL positions in the **CoachCompass®** describe personal perceptions or beliefs; those things that relate to how you perceive yourself.

Who are you? The Initiator position represents your **authentic identity**. The permission to be **you** is typically happening in the beginning or the initiation of your life path; possibly as early as four years of age. By learning the lessons of self-acceptance and personal permission, you are also provided with the opportunity to celebrate yourself authentically to the world.

If you look back at your four-year-old self, how did you see yourself then? Growing up, did you play with dolls or trucks? Did you enjoy creating things or destroying them? Were you the investigator of mysteries, or the leader of the troop? Look back to our example of Will.

> Will was a self-defined advocate for animals. In the Initiator position, this perception allowed him to subsequently pursue interests and make vocational choices that would eventually move him in the direction of working with animals. How do you see yourself?

If you feel that you are currently in the Initiator position, you have an opportunity to learn what excites you; to establish your own personal imprint, acting according to, and in alignment with, your own degree of self-regard. Here you are encouraged to gain the self-assurance needed to be genuine in your actions, making independent decisions most appropriate to your own personal preferences.

Within this position, it is also important to look at your behavior in relationship to your ego. The representation of the ego in this position is reflected in several ways; as being overbearing or defensive of your actions; selfish or needy. Occupying the Initiator is not about getting what you want at the expense of others. Rather, it is about living your authentic life while *honoring* the authentic expression of others.

The Initiator position requires you to define yourself *positively* through independent thought by initiating action; making your own tough choices. In essence, once you have acquired the positive self-regard demanded by this position, it is likely that you will also allow yourself permission to make the necessary critical decisions most important to you over the entire lifetime of your career.

The Initiator position primarily represents certain **Interpersonal Skills** that you may identify with or define while in this position. In general, Interpersonal Skills are the relationship proficiencies that permit personal dexterity; positive interactions with others. Interpersonal Skills in the Initiator position are correlated to your self-perception, your self-esteem and your belief system regarding your own level of self-importance: your **personal role**.

Interpersonal Skills, considered as basic trait competencies, are often best illustrated as you interact through peer, social and environmental involvements. Your level of attention or interest in further developing and using interpersonal skills will also determine your preferences to work alone or work with others; to operate in large work environments or small ones. Recognizing those Interpersonal Skills that you innately possess (positive attitude, optimism) may assist in defining the most appropriate vocational directions/industries in which to succeed with your **preferred skills** as identified in the next position: the Builder.

> Examples of Interpersonal Skills defined for the Initiator Position include: enthusiasm, initiative, assertiveness, etc.

The permission to be, to do and to act begins with personal acceptance. This can happen at any moment in a person's lifetime. If you are at a place in your life where you are truly finding yourself, for the first time or yet again, you are in the Initiator position, embarking on an exciting new voyage of beginnings and independent choices.

The Initiator position requires that we learn to trust ourselves and our own choices, and typically does not exist in one's life without a little heartbreak. At age four, it is likely that you wished to fully be accepted and recognized for who you were. You may have been surrounded by people who were caught up in their own drama of life; possibly over-looking the importance of your need to express yourself genuinely. Were you scolded or supported for wanting to be an artist, a musician or someone out of the ordinary? In the case study of Will, he was fortunate enough to be surrounded by family who were willing to guide his efforts and honor his independent choices. If you were as fortunate as he, then it is likely that you have completed the learning required for this position.

In career maturity, your place in the Initiator position can be a result of years of wanting to, needing to or just breaking free from the past to establish a new, more authentic identity; one that promises to serve your current needs, providing you with a happier life. Self-review requires courage if you are to learn the "Who am I…here and now." The Initiator position encourages you to find the personal power within yourself to make the critical and often unpopular decisions regarding your own needs and requirements.

As you begin charting your career course, you will always begin with the Initiator position. Once you are able to "be yourself," then the question, "How successful do *you* want to be?" can be answered.

Consider these real people *treading water* in the Initiator position:

> Ann does not exhibit a great deal of confidence. Poor self-esteem is apparent. She does not feel that she "fits in."
>
> Andy has been primarily dependent upon other people, living with his family through college and the early part of his career. His parents chose his college education and his career. He hates what he does for a living.
>
> April is in the process of career planning. She has no clue about what she wants to do or what will make her happy.

Here are a few life jackets to get them back into the boat.

Initiator Strategies and Activities:

> Surround yourself with positive people.
> Find a good mirror. (True friends will often be one.)
> Write a personal affirmation. ("I am capable of greater things" is our favorite!)
> Listen to affirmation tapes. (Tony Robbins has some great ones!)
> Do something that allows you to feel personally empowered.
> Create a mission statement for yourself. (Dr. Wayne Dyer is a great resource on the power of intention!)
> Take a course in effective interpersonal communication.
> Paint a picture or make a collage that reflects your unique traits and what you represent.
> Take a personality assessment (suggestions are listed under The Initiator in the Appendix).

Take the "Your Career Check-Up" assessment on our homepage, www.coachcompass.com, to determine whether you are in a Conceptual position.

You have successfully completed the learning required in the Initiator position when you can:

Identify your own personal likes and dislikes.

Recognize and use your positive people skills.

Exhibit independent thought through actions.

Make your own tough decisions.

Exhibit positive self-regard, without ego.

Initiator Preferred Environments:

Consider vocational environments where:

You can feel passionate about the work.

Rote or scheduled activities are continually reviewed.

Job responsibilities are aligned with how you see yourself.

Patience and positive feedback is available while you learn new skills.

You can get excited about going to work.

Avoid environments where:

The job requires that you master new skills daily.

The job requires that you manage or supervise others.

The job is unsupervised; regular feedback is unavailable.

The job is not in alignment with your personal perception of yourself.

In review—

The Initiator is a conceptual position in the planning of one's career. As a conceptual position, it pertains to how you feel about yourself. Positive self-regard is one of the benefits that can arise from spending time revisiting what is really important to you. Once you have fully realized who you are, your actions will be more on track, aligned with your own personal choices. The Initiator position, in essence, allows you to tap into your own personal power to make the choices right for you…your authentic and true self.

So, whether you have succeeded in learning the lesson of the Initiator position in your career, need a refresher or are still struggling with it, the Initiator position is all about identifying a passionate, self-directed role on your stage of life; defining your career through your individuality, as represented by your style, dress, personal affect, language and intention.

Can you see yourself clearly or do you feel lost in a sea of choices that mean nothing to you? If you are seriously planning your course, there is much work to do. Need help? Seek the guidance of a wise coach or mentor.

Are you presently The Initiator?

Creating a strong sense of self-esteem is important to you at this time. You may be at the beginning of your career or creating a brand new direction. Career planning, defining personal preferences, and celebrating your independence from others are the critical themes in this position.

The Second Degree of Learning: What I Do

The Builder

Your talents make you special, and that is why it is important to recognize and develop them. The Builder allows you to take "the valuable you" as identified in the Initiator position and develop skills toward the specific areas of your personal strengths. The Builder is a CONCRETE position addressing tangible skills/competencies that you innately possess and must continue to develop. These skills ultimately will comprise your complete career and life inventory. Why CONCRETE? Primarily, all CONCRETE positions in the **CoachCompass®** describe tangible things; those things that can be measured. This second position in the Career Planning stage represents identification and commitment to your **talent inventory**.

What is it that you do? Your talent inventory comprises the entire suite of vocational skills that you choose to use and/or develop once you understand where your skill preferences lie. You are therefore developing and expanding skills that you innately like or tend to perform well. Chances are that when you were playing with those dolls or trucks, there were certain things that you and others noticed that you were doing well. You may have enjoyed a level of satisfaction in doing them; targeting school or after-school activities to further develop those areas of specific vocational interest. The Builder position allows you to define the ideal vocational inventory and secure it as your career cornerstone.

Through the development of your preferred skills, you are both rewarded and celebrated. Putting energy and effort into activities that you like and do well will also enhance your vocational achievement in these areas, as well as solidify and stabilize your future.

Will was focused and determined to be accepted into veterinary school. It took him more than one try. His entrance exam scores, although high, were not competitive enough to move him forward the first, second or third time. Hour upon hour of extra study resulted in final acceptance to the veterinary school of his choice. These scores were the criteria upon which his entire future would be built. In the Builder position, however, he also continuously developed extraneous skills on jobs totally unrelated to animals remaining in alignment with his talents.

The Builder position, as a planner, emphasizes personal strengths as measured through your preferred skills. This position encourages you to be stable and consistent in your vocational choices so you can continue to reap measurable results from your efforts. The Builder position requires the identification of specific vocational preferences; those things that you excel in doing and should continually develop throughout your lifetime.

The Builder position is most directly aligned with and describes **Job Specific Skills**. These include the specific vocational aptitudes that should be identified and developed early; these contribute to your vocational sustenance. Job Specific Skills, as found in the Builder position, are "fixed" skills, often rote, and are the easiest skills to learn and to teach. The results of Job Specific Skills are also the easiest for you or others to measure; developed by repeating a complete process over and over again. When you combine several individual Job Specific Skills together, you have a Job Specific Process.

Examples of Job Specific Skills defined for the Builder position include: basic structured intelligence areas: reading, writing, math, science, music, art, etc. (You may not think of these as being rote, however, when learning the chords of music, or the best way to apply paint to a canvas, repetition is what allows us to eventually go on "automatic" within a job specific process).

If your innate personal preferences (as discovered in the Initiator position), point to certain Job Specific Skills or propensities, then you would most likely wish to spend time where most of your preferred skills could be utilized, continuing to develop these talents over the course of your career life. The demand of the Builder position is to focus on that which you do well, measure the degree of how well you do it, and then continue to further hone your special skills in the direction of your innate strengths.

Job Specific Skills' identification: the detection of your various innate intelligences (see examples in Appendix) all contribute to this critical planning area, permitting correct vocational choices aligned within the most appropriate development paths.

Consider these real people *treading water* in the Builder position:

> Barb is on a quest to gain new skills. Recently unemployed she realizes that her vocational skills are not in alignment with the current needs of her job, but is unsure of how to redirect her educational focus.

> Ben has been attending school "forever." A perfect representation of "education for the sake of education," he has been hesitant to apply his knowledge within the workplace. He is trying to convince his spouse that he should pursue yet another credential.

> Bess is changing jobs and needs transitional job search tools. She wants to develop more appropriate skills that will result in better career choices.

Here are a few life jackets to get them back into the boat.

Builder Strategies and Activities:

Assess and list those activities that you like and do well.

List potential jobs or careers in which your skills could be applied.

Begin a project that will stretch and expand those activities.

Document a list of new things you want to learn.

Take an IQ or EQ test (suggestions listed under The Builder in the Appendix).

Take the "Your Career Check-Up" Assessment on our homepage, www.coachcompass.com to confirm if you are in a Concrete position).

You know that you have successfully completed the learning required in the Builder position when you can:

List all of your vocational skills and aptitudes.

Prove your vocational ability.

Identify your vocational likes and dislikes.

List the additional skills that may be required for your preferred vocational direction.

Determine the best way for you to learn or to gain new skills.

Assess what skills to build continuously.

Builder Preferred Environments:

Consider vocational environments where:

Your work has an immediate, measurable result.

Newly learned skills are directly applied.

Continuous vocational skill-building is a regular part of the job.

The specific uses of your existing skills can be measured and built upon.

You can identify your talents through your work.

You would not benefit in environments where:

The job limits the use of your preferred skills, abilities or talents.

The job offers nothing that you like doing.

The job limits your access to an expert, mentor or coach from whom to learn.

The job does not fully use your talents.

In review—

The Builder position is a concrete position in the planning of one's career. You are building upon your preferred skills/strengths, applying these talents according to what you wish to do. While in this position, identify and solidify a foundation of skill resources for your continuing career needs.

It is the combination of who you are (the Initiator) and what you do well (the Builder) that will result in effectively planning your preferred direction. Whether you are new in your career or planning to fill skill gaps in the existing one, the Builder is a position of defining yourself through your aptitude, measured as talents and strengths that are unique and special. If your career is somehow derailed, revisit your present inventory to ensure that it is current with the skill sets required for your field of interest. If you are looking to an entirely new direction, a skills check-up is in order for identifying and developing the new skill areas that you may need.

Are you presently The Builder?

Building new skills and measuring your vocational inventory are important to you at this time. You may be early in your career or needing to assess your present skills, determining their best vocational application. Career foundation, vocational inventory, and talent identification are the critical themes of this position.

The Third Degree of Learning: What I Want

The Advancer

Your major career dreams and desires begin in the Advancer position. Deciding what you want is based upon identifying the right fit: preferred lifestyle, work rhythm and vocational environment. The Advancer is a CREATIVE position of **preferences** as identified through diverse experiences. Why CREATIVE? Primarily, all CREATIVE positions in the **CoachCompass**® describe experiential opportunities; the expansion of ideas and concepts. This final position in the Career Planning stage represents defining what you want from your career as discovered through your experiences.

What do you want? Once you have decided who you are and what you excel in, it is time to start applying what you have learned to a variety of environments. You will do this in order to choose which of these will offer the best fit and provide what you want from a job. If you are beginning your career, logically you will need to gain experiences in multiple environments, so as to have a menu of options or choices to select from. Experiencing multiple work options also allows you to narrow your final choices to a certain path or direction through the process of elimination. The Advancer position is all about discriminately choosing among these opportunities; advancing to work environments most appropriate to your personal preferences and preferred talent areas.

Choosing the appropriate educational and experiential environments in which to direct your career path often requires facing the tough choices of a college education. How do you choose the courses that will ultimately provide the career that you want? This decision often requires independent researching of different work environments while you are still in high school.

In retrospect, Will could have applied his interest to a number of potential directions involving animals. As the grandson of farmers, he could have returned to the farm. He could have decided to work for a zoo or started a horse breeding business. In the Advancer position, he reached his ultimate and final choice of career direction only after getting involved in various animal-related activities, then choosing the most interesting environment.

The Advancer position represents the concepts or ideals of a vocation identified and selected through the process of attending school, expanding life experiences, acquiring credentials, or moving through traditional rites of passage. Your best fit is predominantly determined by your personal interests. Your ability to use your preferred skills to make independent choices as based upon personal preferences will help identify which work and life experiences are of most interest to you. In essence, you are learning (through the Advancer position) the degree of certainty in which you will eventually express your authentic self through your work.

The Advancer position emphasizes **Transferable Skills.** More complex than Job Specific Skills, Transferable Skills are developed through multiple work and life experiences. Transferable Skills by their very nature are portable and can be transferred to various vocational or work environments. Correlating to functions or processes, these skills are relevant to many jobs. More difficult than Job Specific Skills to tangibly measure, Transferable Skills are in high demand in professional arenas. As a result, you will find that Transferable Skills can take longer to learn, and are best acquired and expanded by applying these skills in a variety of creative applications.

Examples of Transferable Skills for the Advancer Position include: planning, grouping, categorizing, selecting, etc.

Think of the Advancer as a position that allows you to better define the best career destination from a menu of potential career *ports* as you decide to set sail in a specific direction.

Consider these real people *treading water* in the Advancer position:

> Carey is a "little fish in a big ocean" wherein opportunities to learn, grow and be mentored by others are among the possible choices. She needs to first clarify her preferred career direction.

> Carl is in the early stages of his career considering numerous job opportunities. He feels at a total loss when he is offered more than one job and cannot decide which to accept.

> Cody has bounced from job to job without clear focus. With a tendency to see too many possibilities, he has fragmented his efforts in multiple areas, rather than focusing on a specific goal and gaining the experiential requirements. As the stereotypical "jack of all trades, master of none," he struggles with personal self-discovery.

Here are a few life jackets to get them back into the boat.

Advancer Strategies and Activities:

> List any potential work environments you most would enjoy supporting; available on either a paid or volunteer basis.
> If you are working, find a volunteer opportunity to learn/apply your skills in new environments.
> If you are not working, find paid or volunteer opportunities to apply your skills in a new way.
> Read: *Oh, the Places You'll Go!* by Dr. Seuss.
> Document an "I am…" list, an "I can…" list, and justify the "places to go."

Take an interest inventory (suggestions are listed under The Advancer in the Appendix).

Take the "Your Career Check-Up" Assessment on our homepage, www.coachcompass.com to confirm if you are in a Creative position.

Note: Rarely does the online scoring of **"Your Career Check-up"** as posted on our website, result in a tie. If it does, please retake the assessment a day or two later to resolve the problem.

You know that you have successfully completed the learning required in the Advancer position when you can:

Transfer prior vocational experiences into interesting new work environments.

Tap into multiple life experiences to choose the ones that interest you most.

Identify your personal ideas and apply these concepts to job/work interests.

Identify a realistic career direction.

Create a career plan based on personal preferences, skills and prior experiences/interests.

Advancer Preferred Environments:

Consider vocational environments offering:

Variety and discovery

Several career paths

New work experiences

Internship or mentored positions

You would not benefit in environments where:

The job is rote and single-sided.

The job offers limited growth or career options.

The job limits experiential learning; offers only one vocational application.

The job does not continually stimulate your interest.

In review—

The Advancer is a creative position in the planning of one's career. As a creative position, it pertains to how completely you experience your life, defining your workplace interests. This position requires you to try on "many hats" to see which ones offer the best fit; expanding your experiential horizons in order to better define your ideal career direction.

If the Builder position emphasizes your vocational needs, the Advancer chooses the specific destination for applying those talents. Your life experiences ultimately point to interests that engage you the most, and spotlight your choices on the environments most aligned with those interests. Once you have undertaken various internship or educational opportunities, it will be much easier to address the overwhelming task of defining your direction on paper with a complete career plan.

Are you presently The Advancer?

Discovering new experiences; expanding concepts and ideas are important to you at this time. You may be early in your career, considering advanced educational or experiential avenues, or planning a new career direction. Career options and activities that allow you to define yourself through future possibilities are the critical themes of this position.

Career Planning: In Review

Career Planning encompasses all of the actions required to initiate, solidify and define a viable career direction; engaging in the personal self-discovery required for the documentation of a sound career plan. Each degree or position provides you an opportunity to define yourself through personal introspection, your preferred skills and abilities, and your unique interests.

Career Planning Exercise #1

1) Using the Skills Wheel Sheet found in the Appendix (after the Advancer worksheet), list five People Skills, five Transferable Skills and five Job Specific Skills that you would like to apply to a career. Use the skills reference lists (found under The Builder worksheet) to assist you.

2) Once you have completed Part One of the above exercise, compose a mock resume using the information in each of these three areas. This mock resume will identify a potential profile for the job you would most prefer to do.

The mock resume should include all of the learning accrued in the first three positions:

1) **Who you are:** Personal identifiers.
2) **What you do:** Vocational abilities.
3) **What you want:** Preferred career or work environments.

OFF COURSE: #1

The Skills Wheel: A Tool for Planning and Developing Your Career

The Skills Wheel is a classification tool that was originally developed and used for many years by the Federal government. It was created to allow the identification of the critical competency (skills) areas required for the classification of employment. The three primary areas of the Skills Wheel are people, data and things (functions); these remain the foundation for all of the labor classifications in the United States.

As each job in the United States uses the basis of the original Skills Wheel to define its makeup, it is no surprise that the jobs held or created within the United States are designed to map back to these three core areas of competency. You will notice that these areas have already been addressed within the first three positions of Career Planning and are aligned with all 12 positions on the Career Lifecycle. You can easily correlate them in this way:

> **Interpersonal Skills** relate to your people skills. These skills affect how you connect to others and others connect to you. Knowing your personal preferences for work relationships will determine with whom you will work and how you will work with them.

Job Specific Skills relate to data/information/facts. These are the skills that you can measure and connect directly to the specific job that you are performing. These will also dependably measure your abilities, value, results and impact as these are applied within the workplace.

Transferable Skills are portable competencies or proficiencies that you can develop and expand upon throughout a lifetime of various experiences. Adapting these skills to support a variety of different work environments assists in increasing your potential career options.

Use the graphic worksheet to list your competencies in each area.

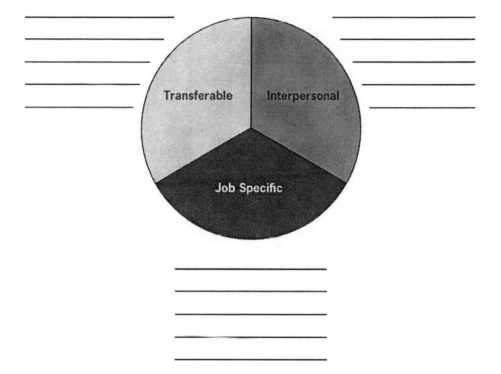

OFF COURSE: #2

Trends: What You Don't Know Will Hurt You!

Before you go further, it is important to note the many changes in the workplace climate that may impact your career planning. As the straight line of the career now comes with curves, new challenges in the workplace may well derail your career choices before you are able to enact them. These workforce shifts may require you to start a new career plan altogether in midstream.

Interview people and ask them how they "landed" in their careers. Many will tell you it was more about luck or getting *shipwrecked* than it was about planning well. The option of uncertainty is not one typically preferred by most people. Therefore it is important to be aware of the changes that may affect the future of your career while you are actually planning for it.

The challenges addressing global business issues are actually driving your hand to be more intentional in planning your career strategies. Within three primary workforce areas: the hiring process, the training and development process, and the retention process, new career challenges continue to be increasingly complex as the age demographics shift within today's workforce.

Consider the landscape of the present work environment. Keep current on its trends as you continue to plan and build upon your career. Here are several examples of some changes that have affected the generic workplace over the last decade.

Hiring—

How you are hired into a job has changed drastically over the last ten years. Most recruiting and hiring is conducted online, with a minimum of positions still being placed in print. This online employment process will continue to change the way that you position yourself in your career. Your ability to network directly with potential employers will greatly improve your chances of multiple and optimal job options.

Training and Development—

How you are trained on the job has shifted to a continuous, self-directed learning model. Classroom training in companies has morphed to computer-based, blended and online training venues. Continuous learning in this way will change the expectation of your job performance in the workplace, also impacting your ability to remain marketable and flexible.

Retention—

How your relationship is initiated and continued with an employer has changed from the employee-employer relationship to predominantly co-employment or contracted work. In 2010, it is projected that the majority of working people, when asked about their employer status, will name "self." This new co-employment relationship rocks the job security notion that once was ideal for some; permitting flexibility in competitive positioning for others.

Put simply, there always will be predictions and trends requiring career adjustments, compelling you to be aware of your place in the changing workplace environment. The most critical change to the workplace will occur in the next 20 years. It is estimated that two-thirds of the workforce will hover over the age of fifty by 2008, and fewer than 50 percent of available workers will replace them as they retire. There is a drought expected in the global workplace with a "body shortage" magnitude not seen in 600 years of work. This scarcity of people and skills available for the workplace will impact workplace balance, commerce and *you* in a variety of ways. The four major predicted impacts of the age shift include the following:

Are you planning to retire?

> Eligibility for retirement is predicted for a large majority of the workforce in a relatively short time period. Unlike previous generations who have retired somewhat permanently, this most recent group will likely (have to) reinvent themselves and may (have to) re-enter the workforce primarily for economic reasons. This expected journey from retirement and into a potential new vocational life will also require new workplace skills and new plans. Predictions have suggested that this retiring workforce may tend to reinvent their lives in many new work directions, inclusive of non-traditional work endeavors.

Will you need to re-enter the workforce or reinvent your career?

Are you seeking promotion?

> The leadership assumption or "progression before its time" is predicted in the younger (mostly unmentored and unprepared) ranks of workers. Vying for leadership positions in the vacuum of the exiting seniors, few will be prepared for what they may face. A colossal challenge for organizations lies in the development of this succession group as the existing workplace may require infrastructure re-creation to accommodate this transition.

Do you have the skills to move into a leadership role prematurely?

Are you open to a new work role?

> Along with the "body" shortage, a "skills" shortage will cause the workplace to become increasingly flexible. Begun in Europe and expanding to the United States, the trend is to NOT be employed, but rather be co-employed or contracted for any work required. This shift from employment to co-employment will require a competent, performance-driven and competitive "just-in-time" workforce requiring a completely different mind-set. Many contractual companies will offer education to their workers to keep their skills current.

Are you ready to work without the "net" of security?

Are you able to articulate and represent your true value?

> Greater workplace fluidity; a global system of work with economies at risk, contractual work on the rise and job growth expecting to double in the next decade will prompt the companies of the future to place the greatest emphasis on performance outcomes achieved by the fewest of workers.

Can you represent your true value accordingly in the marketplace?

Are you prepared to make the right decisions for you?

> These changes will require everyone in the workplace to be better prepared to make the right decisions. As individuals learn to keep up with the consistent changes in their shifting work environments, companies will identify more ways to retain talent to sustain their business.

Take a brief check-up from the neck up in your Career Plan—

Identify and document what you need to sustain, redirect or begin your career. How appropriate is your comfort level in making the right decision now? Do you have the skills that will be required for the "next generation" of work? Do you have a plan in place that will assist you in setting a strong course for your career success?

See if you can complete the **Career Coach Positioner** located in the Appendix.

CHAPTER TWO

Stage Two of the Career Lifecycle

Developing within Your Career

Career Development: the affiliation, marketing and optimization of the career.

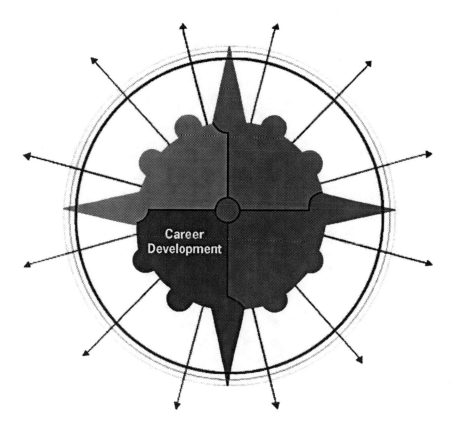

In this stage, you are learning how to position your role in your job and your industry; promoting your professional potential to others, critically observing and redirecting your choices toward your long-term career goals. If you have taken all the correct steps to develop your career well, it is highly likely that you will also be able to transition your career well when any new workplace changes occur. Career Development permits you to answer the question, "When I know what I want, how will I get it?"

Career Development shifts your energies into new areas. Expanding beyond your personal needs into the needs of the workplace, Career Development is about securing your relationship in *any* work environment, presenting your value through career progressions, and optimizing your job opportunities.

As with Career Planning, Career Development is comprised of three distinct positions or degrees. These positions relate to:

> **Who you are**; the professional role you play.
> **What you do**; the professional value you offer.
> **What you want**; the professional risks and job re-direction you consider.

If these examples remind you of similar information assigned in Career Planning, you are correct. Each one of the four stages will repeat the same three generic positions of: who you are, what you do and what you want. The first position in the Career Development stage is the **Nurturer** position.

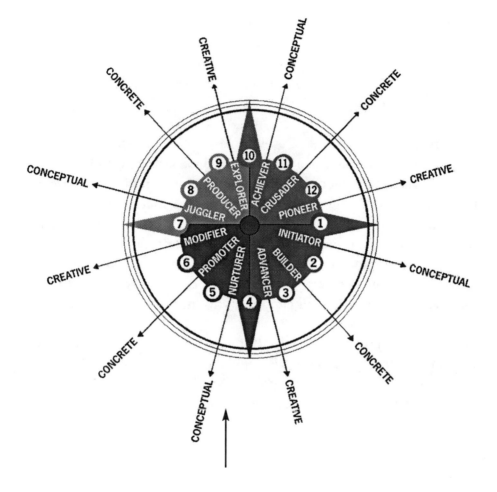

The Fourth Degree of Learning:
What I Represent

The Nurturer

Your reputation is one of the most important commodities within your career portfolio. How you are perceived within work will provide you with unlimited opportunities or a locked door. The Nurturer is a CONCEPTUAL position defining your **professional work role**. This is "what I represent."

The first position in Career Development speaks to the role perpetuation of your professional image, with a primary emphasis on how you place and maintain yourself within the membership of the work environment. You are required to learn skills that may assist you in the development of your reputation or character. The Nurturer position represents work continuity as referenced by your ability to remain in one reliable *role*. As you were defining your personal identity in the Initiator position, here you are learning to establish your **professional identity** as it fits within your chosen environment.

The Nurturer position, like the Initiator position, requires that you expand your **Interpersonal Skills** applied to establish/maintain positive memberships in organizations, groups, teams or clubs. These skills will also allow for the continuance of your professional identity in times of career uncertainty. Develop skills to effectively network; identify strategies for working well in a group; use your affiliations/connections to the best end; establish the ideal reputation.

> Examples of Interpersonal Skills in the Nurturer position include: teamwork, collaboration, networking, etc.

As an extension of the personal self-acceptance that occurred in the Initiator position, the Nurturer position allows the degree of learning required for optimal professional acceptance.

Consider these real people *treading water* in the Nurturer position:

> Denise is a loner. She has learned to make her own way. At work she has been overlooked for promotions and continues to believe that the "old" way of doing things is the best although it has not achieved the results that she has been seeking in her career.

> Darien has had difficulty due to interpersonal conflicts at work. This has been the issue at every job he has held. He is presently looking for a new job again where he doesn't have to be a *team player*.

> David has an established reputation that he has perpetuated in the same workplace for a very long time. He has just lost his job and is having difficulty "seeing himself" working for another company.

Here are a few life jackets to get them back into the boat.

Nurturer Strategies and Activities:

> Establish membership in organizations, groups, teams or clubs.
> Become an adjunct member of a new work team.
> Join an association; actively network at the events.
> Identify opportunities to sit on an organization's board.
> Interview colleagues on their personal view of you; discover your **real** reputation.
> Take a role assessment (suggestions listed under The Nurturer in the Appendix).

You know that you have successfully completed the learning required in the Nurturer position when you can:

Identify and operate as a true member in any workplace culture.

Exhibit positive work habits when relating to others.

Perform your chosen role in your desired work environment, on a team.

Create an ongoing list of networking contacts inside and out of your present work environment.

Transfer your work reputation from one work environment to another.

Nurturer Preferred Environments:

Consider work environments where:

The role of the job and the role in the organization are clearly defined.

Cross-divisional relationships can be developed over time.

Adherence to organizational culture is encouraged.

Appropriate organizational professionalism is required.

Developing and maintaining positive relationships is supported.

You would not benefit in environments where:

The work conducted involves constant role changes and challenges.

The work conducted is ambiguous and requires constant re-adaptation.

The work conducted lacks a clear, succinct, established role in the company.

The work does not allow access to multi-tiered work relationships.

In review—

The Nurturer is a conceptual position in the development of one's career. As a conceptual position, it pertains to how you see yourself in relationship to your work role, your work group, and the work environment; how others regard you as a team member. While in the Initiator position, you identified your authentic, independent self. In the Nurturer position, you are developing your professional self in order to achieve the goal of workplace inclusiveness. This is a position of developing through your professional image: correlating success within the work community as achieved through the acceptance of others. Can you see your role clearly in relation to your workplace?

Are you The Nurturer?

Belonging to a group or association, establishing membership, and creating a beneficial professional role is important to you now. You may be early in your career or shifting to new work environments. Career affiliation, networking and broadening your own reach are critical themes of this position.

The Fifth Degree of Learning: What I Promote

The Promoter

Thriving people know how to "toot their own horn." You can learn to persuade, influence and prove your value within your chosen career. The Promoter is a CONCRETE position personifying your **professional value** as measured through your career progression. This is "what I promote."

This second position in Career Development represents competitive action, as you are seeking appropriate rewards, vocational recognition, and career mobility. The Promoter position encourages you to learn the skills required to "get ahead"; to be seen as a person that contributes great value. Your skills are being demonstrated, proven and represented fully in all that you do. Developing the required marketing skills to promote your professional value is the requirement of this position. Marketing yourself requires the creation of both written and verbal tools that can continually prove your value. The Promoter position is most directly aligned with the **Job Specific Skills** including the specific vocational aptitudes that you will need for continued career progression.

> Examples of Job Specific Skills in the Promoter position include: broad persuasive communication skills, e.g., writing a career portfolio, creating a target market profile; composing resumes, cover letters, thank you letters, and marketing letters; articulating your value through interviews and presentations.

For this position, you are encouraged to be persuasive, influential and accurate in representing who you are, what you do, and what you want so that others can place value on your capabilities. As you begin to measure the reasons why you are of value, you are also learning to provide the tangible "proof" of why you deserve consideration for employment, development or promotion in the eyes of an employer.

Emphasizing your accomplishments and creating a sense of indispensability are themes suggested by this position.

If your personal talents (as discovered in the Builder position) are to have immediate and measurable results, when you find yourself in the Promoter position you exert the effort to compose the resume, send it and *expect* to get the interview.

Consider these real people *treading water* in the Promoter position:

> Edward has a strong drive for career mobility based upon sheer determination. Highly competitive, he relishes the *race* and loves the recognition given for his accomplishments.

> Emily fears failure. She lacks the ability to promote her value to her present employer and, as a result, often feels overlooked, slighted or out of place.

> Enid drives the action. She requires constant public recognition, approval and support from others, but cannot justify why she has regularly been passed over for promotion.

Here are a few life jackets to get them back into the boat.

Promoter Strategies and Activities:

> Document your accomplishments daily: measure these in concrete terms.
> Refrain from being "all talk and no action."
> Keep an ongoing accomplishment journal.
> Involve yourself in a competitive sport or hobby.
> Solicit reference letters regarding your concrete work performance.
> Document a list of potential upwardly mobile opportunities you would like to pursue.
> Take a course in marketing.

Take a marketing assessment (suggestions listed under The Promoter in the Appendix).

Compose a resume with your accomplishments, written out in complete details including measurable areas such as timeframes, percentages, etc. Use persuasive terms like "reduced," "increased," "solved," or "amended" to reflect your ability to measurably impact your work environment.

You know that you have successfully completed the learning required in the Promoter position when you can:

Communicate persuasively both verbally and in writing; influencing others through your words/actions.

Identify realistic opportunities for promotion and advancement.

Measure the value of your efforts to the team, the organization and the customer.

Create a Target Market Plan to direct your efforts to meet the interest level of the audience.

Promoter Preferred Environments:

Consider work environments where:

Challenge and accomplishment is a typical part of the job.

Promotion or progression is possible.

High-level organizational/industry visibility is possible.

Professional exposure for your job is the norm.

Awards and recognition are public.

You would not benefit in environments where:

The work conducted is invisible or lacks challenge.

The work conducted limits your ability to persuade or influence.

The work conducted is stagnant, without any clear promise of progression.

The work does not highlight your career.

In review—

The Promoter position is a concrete position pertaining to how well you can document and articulate your professional value to others. When in the Builder position, you identified your talents. In the Promoter position, you are promoting the value of your talents within the marketplace. Whether you are new to your career or wanting expeditious career progression, the Promoter requires that you continually "log in" your accomplishments and effectively articulate your professional capabilities. This is a position of developing your career through self-promotion. If your career is somehow derailed, you may find yourself revisiting your accomplishment list; re-working the relevancy or representation of these accomplishments as they are applied to a new direction or a new job.

Are you The Promoter?

Promoting the career: measuring your professional value through career movement is important to you now. You may be early in your career, wanting to get ahead or wanting proof or approval of your workplace value. Career progression, personal recognition, and self-promotion are critical themes of this position.

The Sixth Degree of Learning: What I Evaluate

The Modifier

Knowing when to leave one job for another requires the ability to observe, evaluate and mitigate risks within your choices. You can feel much more in control and in charge by continually finding ways to improve your circumstances, then redirecting your actions. The Modifier is a CREATIVE position defining **job re-creation** acquired through the enhancements or improvements of work. This is "what I evaluate."

This final position in Career Development requires you to learn sound observational skills, taking some risks as you employ your critical thinking skills to better your work circumstances. Continually check in on your present location; make certain that it is what and where it needs to be. The Modifier position reflects any necessary improvements, redirecting your decisions and actions as required.

Taking a regular job evaluation or vocational reassessment requires a comfort level for risk. What are you willing to do when you find that you do not have what you want? In the Modifier position, you are learning about refinement. How can your career be refined to better reflect what you need from it? Critical thinking, keen observation, research and detailed planning are the requirements learned while in the Modifier position. These skills contribute to evaluating the evidence; defining required strategies needed to take corrective action. With new action, there always comes change.

There are typically two types of change that may occur throughout your career. The first type is the one that you personally generate. This is called **proactive change**. The second type is the change that is thrust upon you. This is referred to as **reactive change**. Change, in general, is difficult. Whether the change occurs externally from outside elements or you personally generate it, the ability for you to remain flexible in your responses is critical to overcoming any obstacles that may be presented along the way.

The Modifier position recommends learning **Transferable Skills** that correlate to problem-solving functions or evaluation processes, thereby allowing positive results achieved through (preferred) proactive change.

> Examples of Transferable Skills for the Modifier Position include: strategic planning, critical thinking, problem solving, etc.

This position requires you to analyze what is working, what is not, and to identify and employ necessary action strategies to fill the gaps.

Consider these real people *treading water* in the Modifier position:

> Frank is unhappy at work. Certain requirements and structures have developed recently which have caused him to want to make major modifications or improvements in his career. He is willing to take the risks to make these changes.

> Farrah is at the point where a major job change must be made in order to further enhance her career. Her options include: looking for a new position or reinventing her present position.

> Felicia is feeling stuck. This feeling has subsequently limited her work performance, and created a pattern of dissatisfaction felt by her boss and coworkers.

Here are a few life jackets to get them back into the boat.

Modifier Strategies and Activities:

> Ask yourself what you like/do not like about your present job.
>
> List those things that absolutely must change in order for enhancement to occur.
>
> Take courses on evaluation, analysis and problem solving.
>
> Create a detailed action plan to convert your job from its present situation to an entirely new one.
>
> Take a change assessment to see how resilient you are to risk/change (suggestions listed under The Modifier in the Appendix).

You know that you have successfully completed the learning required in the Modifier position when you can:

> Evaluate and assess your present situation.
>
> Identify steps required to enact positive changes.
>
> Take calculated risks while redirecting efforts.
>
> Institute regular quality checks to ensure that you are consistently on track.
>
> Create a detailed evaluation/action plan and implement it based upon observations/evaluations.

Modifier Preferred Environments:

> Consider work environments where:
>
> > Change is a constant part of the job.
> >
> > Critical thinking, problem-solving, and quality initiatives are present.
> >
> > Reasonable risk-taking is an accepted practice.
> >
> > Evaluation and re-engineering of old processes are present.
>
> You would not benefit in environments where:
>
> > The work conducted will never change.
> >
> > The work conducted does not have a quality directive.

The work conducted is institutionalized, bureaucratic or inconsistent.

The work does not allow for needed change or adjustment.

In review—

The Modifier is a creative position in the redirection of one's career. As a creative position, it pertains to how you adjust to what works and what doesn't and what needs to happen next. The demands of this position suggest that you learn to incur small risks to test your comfort level in adapting to these changes. When you were in the Advancer position, you defined your preferred work environments. In the Modifier position, you are considering new job assignments that appear to be more aligned with your present circumstances and needs; modifying that which is no longer working; focusing your energies to optimize your career. This is a position of developing your career through creativity. Your creative competencies are developed by recognizing obstacles or barriers within your job as opportunities for innovation.

Are you The Modifier?

Discovering new ways to do things, analyzing and improving your job situation is important to you now. You may be early or mature in your career, evaluating your present career position. Career enhancement, innovation, and creative decision-making are the critical themes of this position.

Career Development: In Review

Career Development, as found on the Career Lifecycle, is comprised of three positions, each in their own way preparing you to develop an ideal place in your career. Although ideally beginning with your first job, the need to develop your career can occur at any time. Effective Career Development ensures successful membership within a group. Marketing and promotional skills alert others to your talents. Job evaluation puts you in greater control for innovation and creative problem solving, allowing you to take some risks within your present job.

Career Development Exercise #2

Using your list as documented on the Skills Wheel Sheet found in the Appendix, create a new list of three work environments in which your contributions and skills would have optimal professional value. Once you have completed this exercise, compose a mock resume focusing on your role, your value and your ability to adapt to these new work environments.

OFF COURSE: #3

Safe and Secure: The Lesson of the Chicken and the Egg

Before you read any further detail about the lifecycle of your career, you should look at why you can easily get too comfortable in your career choices, especially those that may have been recommended by others. With an entire world out there to discover, why might you choose only the safe *ports*? Perhaps, much like the early sailors, you prefer known waters; however, this myth of job safety may one day serve to sink your ship.

Consider your personal awareness. Do you know what happens around you or do you just trust that everything will continue to be OK? Let us introduce you to the simple illustrative lesson of the chicken and the egg.

Wendy Speaks—

> I grew up living next to my grandfather's retirement farm. It was surrounded by homes and several horse farms just outside the bustling city of Baltimore, Maryland. My grandparents had retired from their working farm in Sykesville, Maryland, to become new residents of Relay, Maryland, a town closer to the main railroad lines of Baltimore City. Their move closer to the city allowed my grandmother to attend nursing school and become one of the first surgical nurses in the state. My grandfather continued farming to provide food for the family. He also

bartered any extra food grown for services and goods. Their younger children, ready to be formally schooled, were promised a better education closer to the city. There were also more job opportunities for the older children. My grandparents had been watching the world around them and decided that it was important to make a drastic change for their family.

As you would expect, my grandfather had chickens on his farm. He collected the eggs every morning, without suffering a scratch. Chickens, as a species, are not particularly "aware," which allows a simple trick to get their eggs. To swap out the fresh eggs without suffering the severe rebuttal of an angry chicken, you follow these steps:

1) Put a wooden egg in the back of your hand.

2) Slip your hand holding the wooden egg under the chicken.

3) Pick up the live egg under the chicken with your front two fingers.

4) Drop the wooden egg from the back of your hand into the nest.

5) Remove your hand from under the chicken.

6) Leave the roost with the live egg in your hand.

The chicken, none the wiser, has just provided breakfast! If you were quick enough in your action, the chicken would not notice the live egg missing, and you would escape with the live egg (and you) totally unharmed.

The lesson of the chicken and the egg demonstrates what my grandparents were teaching their children by changing their lives and moving from the old farm. They paid attention to the changes occurring in the world around them, resisted becoming too comfortable in their ways, and considered the potential opportunities. So what does this have to do with your career?

The workplace has changed drastically over the last two decades. You are no longer promised security or safety; it has become a "survival of the fittest" work world. The "fittest" are those most able to create and maintain a successful career by noticing the small changes occurring around them and responding to these changes accordingly. Those left sitting on the wooden egg will have little ability to *hatch* anything new.

Take a check-up from the neck up in your Career Development—

> Identify and document new skills you will need to sustain or enhance your career. What skills do you need to develop to effectively network, market and redirect your career?

CHAPTER THREE

Stage Three of the Career Lifecycle

Managing Your Career Life

Career Management: the prioritization, fulfillment and potential of a career.

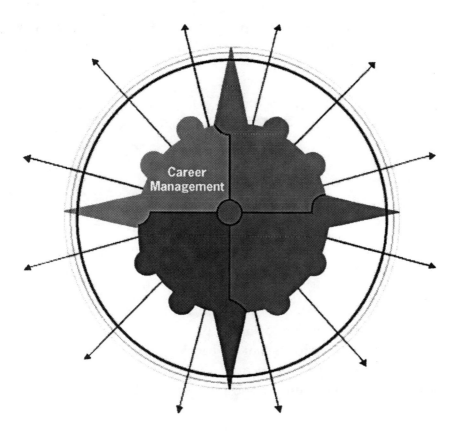

Career Management focuses on how you have manifested and worked your original plan. This stage encompasses the appropriate choices, decisions and actions congruent with your personal and professional values, ultimate career fulfillment, and your work purpose. Career Management "marries" the skills identified during the Career Planning stage to the application and expansion of these skills within the workplace and in your personal life. In the Career Management stage you ask, "Now that I have it, how do I manage it?"

The need to manage your career effectively can occur at any time in your personal Career Lifecycle. Effective Career Management ensures a successful alignment with your personal needs and your professional requirements: work and life, while emphasizing the areas of your work/life priorities, professional victories, and full life potential. Logically, if you did not gain the appropriate understanding and knowledge required to plan your career effectively, then you may encounter many obstacles as you manage it.

As with our previous two stages, Career Management is comprised of three distinct positions or degrees. These positions also relate to:

> **Who you are**: the role you play in your whole life, including career and home environments.
> **What you do**: the access, application and utilization of your resources.
> **What you want**: the alignment of your work to your motivations/principles.

Career Management, as found on the Career Lifecycle, is comprised of three positions, each in their own way preparing you to better manage your vocational and personal choices. Each degree or position provides you with an opportunity to define yourself through your work/life priorities, your resourcefulness, and potential (as discovered by finding purpose within work).

Unlike the Career Planning positions that typically progress in a linear way, the Career Management positions may occur in your life completely out of sequence. When you land in one of these positions, you will need to refer back to the correlating position in Career Planning and assess how well you were able to acquire the learning required there. Accordingly, if you were not successful in gaining the appropriate knowledge required to plan your career well, you may find that you will face many obstacles in managing your present career.

Career Management begins with the **Juggler** position. The Juggler position relies on what you learned about yourself in the Initiator position.

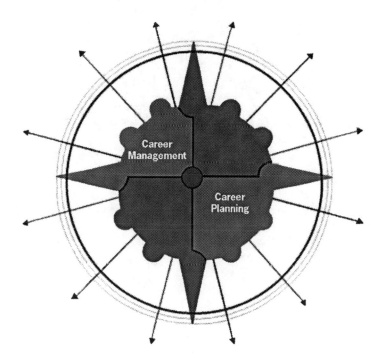

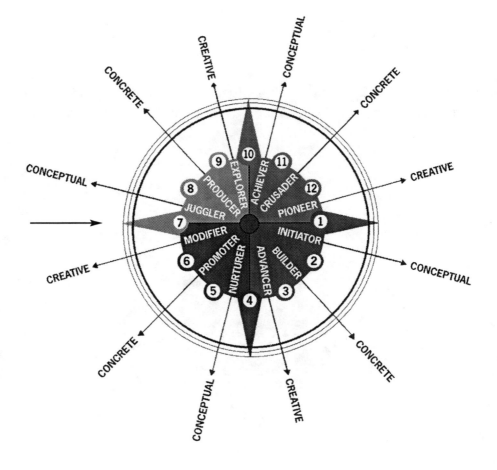

The Seventh Degree of Learning: How I Integrate

The Juggler

We make choices at the beginning of our professional life that suit our lifestyle at that time. Somewhere along the way, things change. It becomes more difficult to determine the priorities. The Juggler is a CONCEPTUAL position defining your perceptions of **self-importance** as you apply them to the choices made regarding home and work. Generated by a change in work/life equilibrium, this is "how I integrate home and work."

The first position in the Career Management stage represents career/life choices or preferences identified in these crossroads. These crossroads arise as your priorities change. When examining the equilibrium of your work and personal life, you may ask, "More work or more play?" How do you make the right choice? Completing additional education or raising a family typically affects your ability to manage your career effectively. As you examine your changing values in home and work life, your actions require conscious management of who you are in relationship to your whole life. The Juggler position reflects your **personal and professional values** as you perceive them in the integration of career/life activities.

In the Initiator position, you were establishing your personal independence and positive self-regard, clarifying the personal preferences that you had for doing some things and not doing others. You may have found it easier to make choices and establish priorities for your actions as long as these choices involved only you. As you mature and expand your life, your relationship with yourself and others changes. The integration of home and work is the challenge in the position of the Juggler.

The Juggler position requires you to learn how to juggle and manage your combined **whole-life identity** within the entire life/work landscape. Your ability to choose the appropriate actions and make the correct decisions in alignment with **actual** rather than the **assumed** needs of both environments often requires determining your own level of self-importance within your home and work roles.

The Juggler position, like the Initiator and Nurturer positions (all conceptual positions), identifies **Interpersonal Skills**. While in this position, you are encouraged to be proficient in integrating home and work, setting appropriate goals that positively affect you and your shared environments and placing appropriate boundaries on what you will and will not do. Prioritizing and planning your time for specific tasks, and increasing your overall organizational and planning skills will allow you greater comfort as you occupy this position.

> Examples of Interpersonal Skills found in the Juggler position include: collaborating, partnering, delegating, assigning, etc.

In this position, you are challenged to take a stand and develop new rules around your own needs as well as the needs of others.

Consider these real people *treading water* in the Juggler position:

> Greg is distracted in his quest to identify the ideal lifestyle, balancing his family life and work. He often over-values his importance by considering himself to be a "super" person who must do it all well.

> Ginny is experiencing career/life imbalance created through constant shifts in priorities within her job. Longer hours have put a stress on her romantic relationship. She is trying to find harmony without allowing others to direct her decisions and actions.

Gary vacillates between wanting more family time and wanting to complete his degree for a promotion at work. He often fails to set goals, and tends to make decisions that please others rather than placing boundaries between certain areas of his life.

Here are a few life jackets to get them back into the boat.

Juggler Strategies and Activities:

Define yourself clearly through the shifting roles that you have created at home and at work.

Create a schedule; determine how to better cluster activities to save time.

Complete a goal sheet for both work and home (see Appendix).

Make a list of things that could be delegated: at work, at home.

Eliminate: make a list of things that are no longer priorities.

Document a weekly priority list of work and home activities.

Take a whole-life value assessment (suggestions listed under The Juggler in the Appendix).

Define the value of the time assigned to each effort, task, and activity.

You know that you have successfully completed the learning required in the Juggler position when you can:

Make appropriate choices/decisions at work and at home.

Set appropriate work/life boundaries.

Adhere to your own values when challenged by work commitments and home events.

Optimize your efforts by delegating or eliminating unnecessary actions.

Create a short- and long-term goal sheet to better plan time and activities.

Juggler Preferred Environments:

Consider career environments that:
> Are grounded in work/life values.
> Permit work/life balance, equilibrium.
> Support healthy home/work relationships.
> Align both personal and organizational values.

You would not enjoy environments where:
> The work expectation is inflexible and rigid.
> The work expectation contradicts your values.
> The work expectation requires massive overtime or limits a balanced life.
> The work expectation does not allow adaptation as the home and work life changes.

In review—

The Juggler is a conceptual position that addresses what is really important in your life. As an extension of the personal acceptance and independent thought that you acquired in the Initiator position, the Juggler position requires you to learn your true whole-life identity, considering the importance that you assign to work and home. Determining your priorities and acting appropriately for the actual (not imagined) needs of the moment are the management skills of this work/life integration. This is a position of managing your whole life by setting necessary boundaries.

Are you The Juggler?

Making the correct choices to integrate work and life is important to you now. You are mature in your career, moving through life changes and struggling with boundaries affecting work and home requirements. Career/life choices, personal values, and priorities are critical themes to this position.

The Eighth Degree of Learning: How I Succeed

The Producer

Orchestrating success may come in the form of starting your own business or operating your department as a profit center. When the time comes to measure your performance through your own definition of success, you will be in the Producer position. The Producer is a CONCRETE position addressing the **success inventory** required for lucrative work experiences as acquired through greater professional clarity, technical mastery and use of complex resources. This is "how I succeed."

The second position in the Career Management stage represents career fulfillment acquired through the results of all prior work and life efforts. As the Builder position addresses your vocational inventory, the Producer transforms this final inventory, making it highly useable so you can apply these resources toward their utmost benefit. Certainly, if you have not developed the skills required to sustain your career successfully, it will be difficult to orchestrate any professional success when you arrive in the Producer position. The Producer position measures your professional performance using the resources you have developed.

As the complement to the Builder, the Producer requires a revisit to your complete asset inventory, targeting the vital, methodical use of this inventory to ensure the ultimate triumph. You could consider this a position of entrepreneurship, utilizing business skills to provide access to, and the appropriate use of, all the resources required to ensure a positive outcome. Through the management of these total resources, you can possibly fulfill your greatest dreams.

The Producer position requires you to effectively facilitate the use of these complete and complex systems, inclusive of people, data and things, employing all of these to optimize your efforts on all levels. The

Producer position is most directly aligned with **Job Specific Skills** which include the specific vocational aptitudes that you will need for this major orchestration.

> Examples of Job Specific Skills in the Producer position include: Resource identification; allocation and assignment, budgeting, business plan development, etc.

The Producer as a Career Management position measures the degree of proficiency in which you realize any entrepreneurial-type accomplishments.

Consider these real people *treading water* in the Producer position:

> Helen enjoys mastering and performing new skills. She is considering an entrepreneurial venture that would bring great reward for her efforts. However, she hates asking other people for help.

> Harvey exhibits a strong desire to succeed, often without completing the pre-work required to set a firm foundation through which success is assured. Prior ventures have come to a standstill because of incomplete resources.

> Henry is going full speed ahead in his new department. This is typical, but he may soon be traveling in reverse. He has no documented plan for his new project.

Here are a few life jackets to get them back into the boat.

Producer Strategies and Activities:

> Document your resources and organize their importance.
> List ways others can provide assistance; contribute benefit to your efforts.

Identify work projects that could fully utilize all of your skills and experiences.

Identify individuals who could benefit from contributing to your efforts.

Take a course on project management.

Take a success assessment (suggestions listed under The Producer in the Appendix).

Compose an access list documenting your people, data and things inventory to reflect your ability to measurably impact your professional goals.

You know that you have successfully completed the learning required in the Producer position when you can:

Set performance standards and adhere to them.

Direct systems/processes and people to achieve goals.

Develop and sustain strategic resource alliances.

Measure inputs vs. outcomes.

Create and implement a professional business plan.

Producer Preferred Environments:

Consider career environments that champion:

Utilization of diverse resources.

Project management.

Performance-based outcomes.

Entrepreneurial or consulting practices.

You would not enjoy environments where:

The work expectation is overly detailed, myopic or limited.

The work expectation is primarily task-oriented.

The work expectation is not results-driven.

The work expectation does not rely on successful performance.

In review—

The Producer is a concrete position in the managing of one's career, pertaining to how you can bring together tangible resources (your complete inventory) in a process (system) to ensure the ultimate career outcome (success as you define it). Likened to the staging of a theatre production, you will need to address and review the big picture as well as facilitate all of the minute details required for a successful "opening night." This is a position of managing your career through systems. If your career is somehow derailed, you may find yourself revisiting your assets inventory (people, data and things) to identify how well this list presently allows you to realize success.

Are you The Producer?

Orchestrating and measuring performance is important to you now. You may be mature in your career, possess an entrepreneurial spirit, or consider starting your own business. Career fruition, synergistic resources/systems, and success achieved through performance are the critical themes.

The Ninth Degree of Learning: How I Investigate

The Explorer

The last of our Career Management positions is the Explorer. The learning that is required when you visit this position is motivational discovery. What drives your actions? This is a CREATIVE position representing **mature career exploration**. It relates to the identification of experiences that will have greatest and most evident growth potential. This is "how I investigate."

Your career potential is fully realized by investigating your purpose within work. You may find that these motivations may have changed as your career life has matured. Career choices that you had considered while in the Advancer position may no longer seem viable. The Explorer position offers the opportunity to revisit why you are where you are, and if you should stay or leave. Discovering your present work motivations, while considering the most appropriate alternatives are in order. You are encouraged to explore your reasons for working a certain job or within a certain environment. Investigating alternative work environments that could more fully meet your needs is the goal of this position. Often referred to as the "raison d'etre" or "reason for being" position, occupying the Explorer position typically signifies that you have outlived your present career life and are off exploring new possibilities.

The Explorer represents **Transferable Skills** required for discovery; demanding that you learn what drives you the most. This is done by revisiting past experiences and identifying those that were most meaningful to you. There is a direct correlation between your motivation for doing something and your level of interest and commitment. As the degree of learning in this position is related to your potential, your fullest potential cannot be realized until you are able to determine the true purpose behind your actions.

Examples of Transferable Skills for the Explorer Position include: investigation, exploration, inspection, scrutiny, etc.

This is a position of engagement and, as such, suggests focusing on your personal and professional reasons for work. Discovering those environments that align with your ethics and philosophies, while permitting unlimited ways to grow, is most desirable.

Consider these real people *treading water* in the Explorer position:

> Ima is defining work that feels right with her life. Her recent job has involved covering for people who under-perform. Overwhelmed with no time to learn new skills, she wants to explore growth opportunities in a new environment that adheres to strong work ethics.

> Inid holds "just a job." She is interested in new career possibilities. She is willing to consider additional education and has approached her employer about new areas of responsibility.

> Immanuel has had no career mobility and has worked only for the paycheck. He recently lost his job and realizes he does not wish to return to the same type of unrewarding work where the customers are often "ripped off" by the company. He would like more from his career than punching the "retirement clock."

Here are a few life jackets to get them back into the boat.

Explorer Strategies and Activities:

> Define what "work" means to you.
> Identify work that is meaningful to you.
> Examine areas of work that would allow you to stretch.
> Take a motivation assessment (suggestions listed under The Explorer in the Appendix).

You know that you have successfully completed the learning required in the Explorer position when you can:

Identify the principles and motivations behind your actions.

Investigate alternative work options.

Align your career with appropriate new growth environments.

Eliminate present experiences that no longer "work" for you.

Create an exploration plan for discovering greater purpose within your work.

Explorer Preferred Environments:

Consider career environments that offer:

Creative alternatives to "business as usual."

Professional development initiatives; cross-functional training.

Translation and expansion of existing skills into new applications.

Immediate growth and regular learning spurts.

You would not enjoy environments where:

The work expectation is exactly the same for everyone.

The work expectation does not have a clear purpose.

The work expectation limits your professional growth.

The work expectation does not align with your principles.

In review—

The Explorer is a creative position in the management of one's career. As a creative position, it pertains to how you review your past experiences and investigate new alternatives more closely aligned with your purpose. Expanding upon the Advancer position, this discovery is based upon both your preferences for certain work environments, and your ability to be fully realized within them. This is a position of managing your career through your principles. Managing your career through your work motivations and personal principles becomes the justification for your work.

Are you The Explorer?

Discovering alternatives to the traditional work experience is important to you now. You may be mature in your career path and desire to fully examine your true career potential. Career/life expansion, redefining the workplace experience, and gaining wisdom are the critical themes.

Career Management: In Review

Career Management, as the third stage found on the Career Lifecycle, is comprised of three positions, each in its own way preparing you to live your life more fully, more abundantly and with greater intention. Typically occurring in career maturity, this stage encompasses all of the actions required for managing career/life equilibrium, realizing success goals and feeling more in tune with your work. Married to Career Planning, the Career Management stage purports that without planning your career well, you may find difficulty managing it.

Career Management Exercise #3

Research and create a wish list of environments in which your values, assets and motivations would be a good fit. Once you have completed this exercise, compose a resume focusing on your preferred life/work role, your ideal life or areas of potential personal and professional growth.

OFF COURSE: #4

Equity

It is impossible to separate the career from the person. The lessons you have learned in your life about your personal value, professional value and self-worth have come from other people. Be sure that **you** place an actual value on your time, your knowledge and your contributions.

The meaning of equity varies, dependent upon the context in which the term is used. Defined here, equity means, "Your just and fair compensation according to your right." Assess your belief about what you are worth in terms of what you have to offer others.

Here is an example:

> Jane works 60 hours a week. Her employer holds her responsible for meeting impossible deadlines. If the deadlines were reasonable, the monetary rewards to the company would not be as great.
>
> Jane is dedicated; willing to work an average of 20 hours overtime without pay on a regular basis. She works on average an additional 50 percent of her total time per week. This is the equivalent of another part-time person.
>
> She is paid $25 an hour for a 40-hour workweek. She believes this to be a great rate. Unfortunately, when it is divided by the actual 60 hours a week that she works, she really makes only $16.60 an hour. She not only loses in direct compensation, but also in indirect compensation reflected through the taxes paid

toward her retirement and the employer-matched contributions to her 401k fund.

Result: By failing to ask for what she is worth to the company, Jane is living from paycheck to paycheck (while she continuously increases the profits of the company). The business always wins.

Why do you think Jane allows this? It could be for a number of reasons. She may fear losing her job if she fails to work overtime. She may feel that she is winning because the employer pays her a hefty hourly rate greater than what she believes she is worth. Ultimately, the employer wins because she is doing the job of 1.5 people. This is not an equitable arrangement.

The lesson of equity considers the value that you offer to the workplace in relation to your compensation at that fair market value. Jane's employer can afford to pay more because they are making more from Jane's contribution. The additional money is available. If Jane asks for more money without proving her value, however, she potentially risks losing her job. It is important for Jane to first recognize her value, then to continuously represent and articulate that value to her employer (or find new employment).

Equity requires a direct reward for the contribution and impact of your efforts as based upon what the receiving party is able to measure. You may be more inclined to allow others to determine your value; however, these individuals really are only able to measure the benefit that you apparently bring to them and not necessarily your true worth.

In business, the bottom line is usually more important than equity. After all, if you are willing to work 60 hours and be paid only for 40, that is your choice. It is interesting that many people complain about what they are paid on their job; however, they originally accepted that pay rate, the conditions of the job and the overtime assigned. (What is wrong with this picture?)

So, how do you assign a value to your work? First, do the research. What is the *going rate*? The going rate is typically assigned for an average performance. Is your performance just average? Where on the scale do you place your optimum contribution? The going rate also considers a reasonable work schedule. Is your schedule reasonable or like Jane's?

In order for you to get back on track with equity, you need to do some homework. Research your profession; determine how your profession best proves its workplace value. For example, if you work in a hospital greeting new patients, how is your job optimized through your efforts? One way could be your positive attitude. Another way could be the level of your paperwork accuracy. What do you do that entitles you to fair compensation? These are the reasons why you bring value to your environment and are worth what you are **worth**. Your value can be measured in several ways:

- **Your interpersonal skills:** How well you adapt, relate to, and get along with others.
- **Your job specific skills:** How adept and proficient you are in your job tasks.
- **Your transferable skills:** How you perform in the overall functions and processes required for the job.

Each one of these three areas should be fully investigated. Write down a list of each describing your special contributions. Consider another example:

Jim is a consultant. He has worked in this capacity for many years. Jim will tell you that he conducts this work because he loves to help people. This is a noble way of looking at it; however, Jim tends to martyr himself through his work, sacrificing his weekends and the freedom to spend time with his family. His clients do not understand that there is work that is done behind the scenes in preparation for the meetings that he attends and the presentations that he gives. His clients constantly complain about tight budgets and yet are consistently rewarded through Jim's efforts, inviting him back. Jim will tell you he has raised his rates a little, still remaining 40 percent below his industry value. He will also tell you that his clients continue to whine about the fees and require him to work weekends for Monday deadlines.

Jim contends that he is just not money-oriented and would not change his lifestyle if he "came into money," yet would like to make "a little more" and would enjoy being perceived as worth it.

Both Jane and Jim need to change their minds and their behaviors. They need to set their own value independent of the opinion of others, while considering the actual benefit that the employer or clients are receiving. Here are several strategies that will assist their efforts and yours in creating equity.

Look first at the habits you have created in relationship to your workplace contribution. If you are not brave enough to change these habits where you are, then be brave enough to find a new employer, and establish new clients. When you find a new employer or new clients, establish the new rules and create new behavior.

Consider this list:
- Articulate the conditions of your work relationship in detail to your employer and to your clients. What are you willing to do? Where, when, how and for what?
- Charge for your actual contribution (personal time, knowledge, proficiency).
- Continuously remind yourself of your value as it contributes directly to their need.

- Continuously remind THEM of your value in measurable terms on a regular basis.

- Present your value to them in measured tangible results rather than conceptual terms.

- Document your actual output and the potential impact on the work, the person, and the organization. (This will also remind you of your own worth.)

- Consider the concept of the "wisdom value" that you bring…just how much would it cost them to replace that "wisdom value"?

- Most importantly, believe that you are truly worth the value you assign to yourself and your work.

Want a raise? Look at these subliminal ways to be perceived differently.

- Change your image. Change your hair, your dress and your behavior.

- Be proactive in your approach by anticipating needs.

- Identify ways that you save the company or the client time, money and effort. These are called "value-adds." Write them down and share them.

- Ask for letters of reference before you need them. Be persistent and insist that these are for your personal knowledge and feedback.

- Remind them of how you have improved (and continue to improve) the level of work performance.

What you give should be what you get. Equity is about contribution and reward, not sacrifice, fear or greed. Once you change your mind about your value, your true worth will be rewarded.

CHAPTER FOUR

Stage Four of the Career Lifecycle

Transforming Your Career Life

Career Transition: Changes within your career.

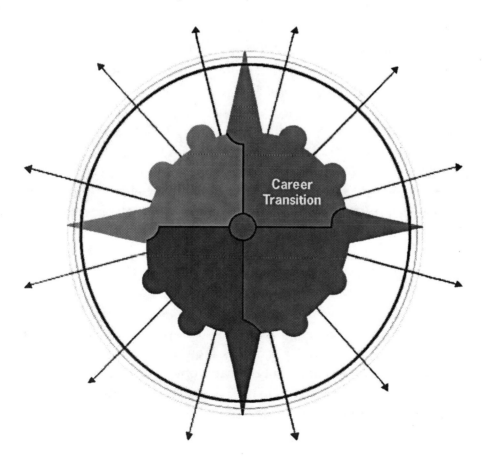

Career Transition encompasses the components of work that relate to achievement, contribution and renewal. This fourth stage addresses the coping competencies required for the successful evolution of a career, including responses/reactions to major changes that may or may not be self-imposed. In this stage you are realizing, "Nothing in my career is guaranteed."

Typically occurring in career maturity, the adjustments required as your career moves through transitions can be overwhelming. Effective Career Transition ensures a successful evolution that supports both your personal requirements within work as well as your professional requirements within your life. Even as your career undergoes changes, this stage relates to:

> **Who you are:** your work role as it evolves and shifts.
>
> **What you do:** your impact: professional contributions.
>
> **What you want:** your complete transformation.

Career Transition as found on the Career Lifecycle is comprised of three positions, each in their own way preparing you to make the necessary changes in your career and life successfully. Each degree or position provides you with an opportunity to define yourself through career triumphs/defeats, professional impact, and retirement/post retirement role.

Similar to the Career Management positions, the Career Transition positions may occur in your career completely out of order. When you land in one of these positions, refer back to the correlating position in the Career Development stage; assess how well you were originally able to acquire the initial learning that was required there. Accordingly, if you were not successful in gaining the appropriate knowledge required to develop your career well, you may find that you will encounter obstacles in the transitioning of it.

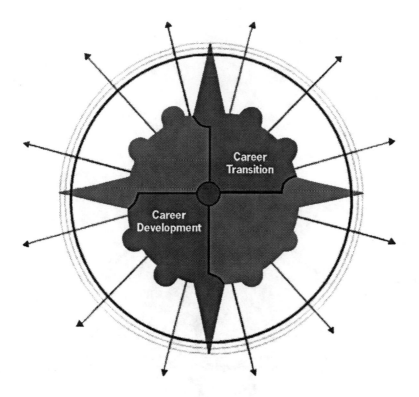

Career Transition begins with the **Achiever** position. The Achiever position relies on what you learned about yourself while meeting requirements in the Nurturer position.

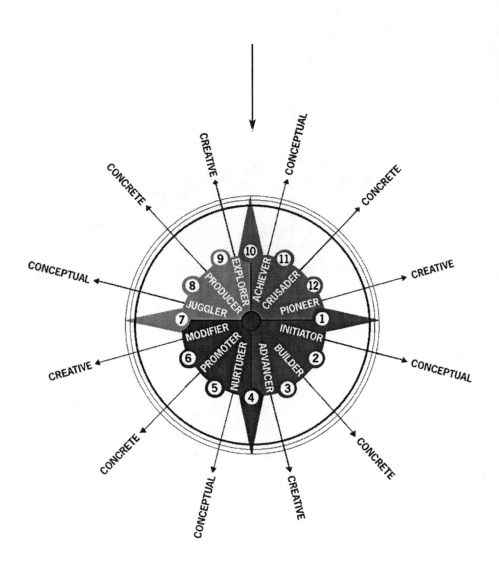

The Tenth Degree of Learning: How I Achieve

The Achiever

Not all of you are achievers in the *driven* sense of the word; however, that said, you still want to be comfortable at each destination on the career journey; whether it means money, power, a new job title or demotion (job loss). The Achiever is a CONCEPTUAL position defining a **respectful professional role** relating to expert status and changes in position hierarchy. This is "how I achieve."

The first position in the Career Transition stage represents changes in your career, reflecting a steady rise in authority and respect, or demotion in status (as in becoming unemployed or retired). This transition may occur over time, be repeated, and is often evidenced by the attainment of credentials, increased levels of work load, or acquisition of greater job responsibility. The Achiever reflects your personal achievement as perceived through your **professional status,** inclusive of workplace behaviors presented and irrespective of actual position assignment or job title.

The Achiever position considers the rights that you feel you have accumulated through your career as a result of a change in job status or work relationships. The ultimate status, however, is one that is reflected by your own self-respect and the respect of others, rather than through the outward symbols of success (house, car, boat, etc.).

The Achiever position, like the complementary Nurturer position, requires that you perpetuate positive work habits that reflect your career responsibly. In this position, you will find that relationships evolve as you rise to new heights, requiring appropriate behavior changes as you progress. New levels of **self-definition,** i.e., how you see yourself and perceive others in relationship to you, will take precedence.

Through achievement, your perception of your job role, interactions with subordinates and major changes in environmental expectations may impact the amount of time and energy required to adapt successfully to any new position or extreme job change. Unfortunately, financial achievement, career status, or a promotion from a "technician to a leader" brings new obligations. Working long hours, driving others to reach their personal best, and living up to the level of your own ambition may wear heavily on you. Conversely, you may have to (gracefully) forfeit your earned authority and entitlement, particularly if you find yourself unemployed. Your self-respect, however, should never be compromised by the status of unemployment.

The learning in this position emphasizes creating and sustaining positive and productive relationships no matter *where* you are within the hierarchy. This includes embracing healthy views of your work and associated rewards. Through the development of interpersonal skills required to address this accommodation, reasonable work habits will permit you to set sensible limits on the expectations of any position, person or circumstance (including yourself). The Achiever position further considers **Interpersonal Skills** that contribute to your association with other people irrespective of **their** placement in the work environment.

> Examples of Interpersonal Skills in the Achiever position include: respect, appropriate treatment of others, leadership skills (delegation, mentoring), etc.

As an extension of the professional reputation initiated in the Nurturer position, the Achiever position demands professional self-respect while also maintaining respectful work relationships along the way.

Consider these real people *treading water* in the Achiever position:

Judy is very ambitious and is committed to achievement as the sole goal, yet her success is being jeopardized by her outdated relationships to the work and people. She is a workaholic; her drive has created a loss of respect for herself, family, friends, colleagues, rules and systems. She achieves by stepping on, over and around people and things.

Jarad has risen to a position beyond his aptitude and interest, i.e., the technician who became the manager, and is challenged to find any personal comfort in his new leadership position. He treats his former peers as "buddies" to the dismay of his superiors.

Jim has been demoted. Rather than engaging in productive activities, he chooses to continue his old, inflexible behaviors at work. He is at risk for early retirement, and says he no longer feels the need to stay informed or current, yet expects peers and subordinates to treat him with respect solely on his tenure.

Here are a few life jackets to get them back into the boat.

Achiever Strategies and Activities:

Identify a role model. List the distinct personal characteristics that make this individual's career position appealing.

Showcase your talents and skills in an authoritative or expert role.

Identify someone to mentor.

Interview peers and gather feedback on your leadership skills.

Retain your position of self-respect by volunteering if you find yourself unemployed.

Take a leadership assessment (suggestions listed under The Achiever in the Appendix).

You know that you have successfully completed the learning required in the Achiever position when you can:

Clearly define your present role in relationship to your whole career.

Adapt improved work habits to achieve *realistic* goals.

Assume a new role; receive respect through your work.

Create/maintain respectful and appropriate work relationships with colleagues.

Create a vision statement regarding your new position.

Achiever Preferred Environments:

Consider career experiences where:

Respect is relegated to all levels of hierarchy.

Mentoring others is a regular part of your job description.

Status is gained/sustained through positive leadership actions.

Expert status is consistently developed and rewarded.

You would not benefit in environments where:

Your area of expertise is hidden and unimportant.

Your area of expertise limits the level of achievement you can acquire.

Your area of expertise is becoming obsolete.

Your area of expertise lies within organizational uncertainty.

In review—

The Achiever is a conceptual position in the transition of one's career. As a conceptual position, it highlights how you perceive your work relationships as you acquire new levels of achievement and attainment. The Achiever position encourages you to recognize what is required to appropriately redefine your role as the work relationship changes. This is a position of transitioning effectively by honoring your workplace and whole-life obligations. Expanding upon the professional role first established within the Nurturer position, the Achiever position typically makes itself known as a result of entitlements and losses in the career. As the level of your membership changes, you are charged with embracing the positive achievement symbols (respect, reputation) throughout the changes.

Are you The Achiever?

Symbols that represent status, authority, entitlement or accomplishment are important to you now. You are mature, transitioning in your career, and have a certain level of expectation/obligation regarding work hierarchy and achievements. Career reputation, respect, and professional perspective are critical themes.

The Eleventh Degree of Learning: How I Impact

The Crusader

You will find that one of the truest reasons for doing anything in life (including work) is that you wish to be rewarded. The Crusader is a CONCRETE position defining the **rewards of your contribution**. This is "how I impact."

As the second position in the Career Transition stage, the Crusader represents the consequences of your actions. Your present workplace rewards may be under scrutiny. How do you contribute to your environment; what direct benefit do you reap from it? Changes occurring while you occupy this position encourage you to identify the impact you can enact on an environment.

The Crusader position encourages you to learn skills required to tangibly measure your work contribution; "What you give is what you get." Like the Promoter position, where you were learning to express your own marketplace value, in this position, equity holds greatest importance.

Learning the lesson of equity requires that you first realize the value of your personal and professional contribution to the workplace, then determine the appropriate reward that you are due because of this contribution. Is your present reward enough? Too much? If so, then perhaps your time could be allocated to voluntary or alternative work.

The Crusader position is most directly aligned with and describes **Job Specific Skills** including the specific vocational aptitudes that you will need to gain and sustain equity within your work.

Examples of Job Specific Skills in the Crusader position include: performance measurements, workplace negotiations, accomplishments journals, etc.

The Crusader, in a Career Transition position, represents changes that must occur for both you and the environment to "win equally." As you learn to act in accord with mutual benefit, you will expand upon the confident energy of the Promoter position. The Crusader defines your true professional value, and judges the appropriate return as it applies to the overall equation.

If your marketplace value (originally discovered in the Promoter position) is recognized, when you find yourself in the Crusader position, you will be rewarded by it.

Consider these real people *treading water* in the Crusader position:

Kim finds that her ideas are presented before their time. As the trendsetter, she is challenged by an environment that takes her ideas and does not reward her for them.

Karen is disappointed with her work environment yet still wishes to remain a contributor. She makes more money than she feels she deserves, yet finds little satisfaction in her work. Often she feels underutilized.

Kip, nearing retirement, is struggling with a workplace that ignores his years of experience. He wishes that he could contribute his wealth of experience and be fully utilized.

Here are a few life jackets to get them back into the boat.

Crusader Strategies and Activities:

Align yourself with others of similar values, thoughts or directions.

Research the environments that could reward you appropriately for your impact.

Consider public service or volunteer work.

Document personal and professional rewards that you require as absolute conditions of employment.

Identify environments that could offer elements of mutual benefit.

Create a personal rewards profile.

Take an altruistic assessment (suggestions listed under The Crusader in the Appendix).

Compose a list of your most significant work contributions.

You know that you have successfully completed the learning required in the Crusader position when you can:

Identify and validate your personal contributions.

Identify trends that may shift personal and organizational impact.

Measure your direct professional contribution within your organization.

Create changes to your compensation.

Crusader Preferred Environments:

Consider career experiences where:

Accountability is part of the job.

Compensation is directly correlated to performance.

Professional and personal impact are clearly defined, measured and rewarded.

Organizational rewards (bonus programs) are offered.

You would not benefit in environments where:

Your expertise is micro-managed and individual impact is overlooked.

Your expertise is applied to meet limited organizational expectations.

Your expertise is lost in the requirements of the organization.

Your expertise is not rewarded in time, effort, ideas or commitment.

In review—

The Crusader position is a concrete position highlighting how you can measure accountability in yourself and others. While in this position, you should acquire and continuously develop skills that allow the measurement of your personal contribution within your chosen environment and the recompense that you receive in kind. Changes in levels of your personal satisfaction vs. reward will require you to continually define what is most important at the time. This is a position of transitioning your career by understanding the consequences of the work relationship. Your actions and the actions of others are rewarded only through the knowledge that if *this* work is conducted, *that* reward occurs. In the Crusader position you are required to evaluate your present impact and direct changes to get just reward.

Are you The Crusader?

Gaining equity through your work is important to you now. Although altruistic interests may exist, you measure results through personal efforts and appropriate compensation. Career/Life contribution, impact and consequences are critical themes.

The Twelfth Degree of Learning:
How I Reinvent

The Pioneer

You will pull into that final *port* and realize that the career journey has been completed. It may feel like an "all-too-brief" vacation, leaving you totally unprepared for the next adventure. The Pioneer is a CREATIVE position **redefining your whole life** through new experiences. This is "how I reinvent and transform."

The last of the Career Transition positions, The Pioneer position represents complete career/life regeneration, relinquishing the personal and professional life that has gone before and planning an entirely new representation. How do I start over?

Previously, this could be considered to be a position of career retirement; however at present, it is referenced by major changes that affect your life. You could consider this to be the most mature position on the Career Lifecycle. Landing in this position suggests that you should prepare to take the great "leap" to something entirely new. Taking this leap requires detailed planning and a high threshold for risk. All the conditions and requirements of your career and personal life are under scrutiny. A thorough analysis and evaluation of the present climate is in order; wait until you have the full picture to make major decisions. You will in essence be starting again at ground zero in a new direction, but not without sufficient planning needed to leave the current life behind; ensuring benefit in the new one. The Pioneer is the poster child of major life changes. You are urged to identify expansive new goals, and then plan discriminately how to pursue these goals.

As you can well imagine, letting go and taking the plunge requires great risk. If you have found yourself in this position prematurely, it may be due to unexpected job changes that have forced an early retirement.

When you are gaining skills within the Pioneer position, you are learning that taking major risks can pay off as long as you are prepared to cope with the effects of these major changes. How can your career and life be so completely redirected and still provide you with those things you deem important? You will have to scrutinize the requirements and conditions of your present life vs. the requirements and conditions of an entirely new life.

Similar to the Modifier position, evaluating your situation will include a review of personal budgets, finances and preferred geographical locations for living and working. As the Modifier position considers the job change elective, this position views a complete life change as an **absolute** for survival. Subsequently, there may be a strong level of discomfort should this change be imposed upon you. The Pioneer position recommends learning **Transferable Skills** that correlate to the discovery of preferred, yet not previously chosen, modes of living.

> Examples of Transferable Skills for the Pioneer Position include: researching new personal and professional options, financial planning, and retirement planning.

Consider these real people *treading water* in the Pioneer position:

> Lynn is preparing for a leadership position that will be a total shift in her career. This change will also require her to move to a new country, embrace a new culture.

> Larry is attempting to launch into a totally new career direction. He is quitting his old job before completely researching what his new career will entail.

> Lou is leaving his old life behind and completely changing both his personal and career environments. A stockbroker on Wall Street, he likes to cook in his spare time and wants to open a restaurant in the mountains of Colorado.

Here are a few life jackets to get them back into the boat.

Pioneer Strategies and Activities:

>Plan BEFORE you leap.
>
>Join a networking or support group; reinvention requires knowing all the obstacles and benefits of the new journey.
>
>Learn something completely new; this often allows you to view yourself in a completely new light.
>
>Get professional help with those things that others could do better: a good financial planner, a good realtor, a good career coach, etc.
>
>Take a retirement assessment to see how open you are at this major stage (even if you are not retiring) listed under The Pioneer in the Appendix.
>
>Create a detailed new life plan; include all of those items that ensure both personal and professional comfort, and then implement it.

You know that you have successfully completed the learning required in the Pioneer position when you can:

>Creatively reconstruct your life, both personally and professionally.
>
>Adapt, be flexible and embrace whole-life changes.
>
>Visualize end-results; map strategies to meet new goals.
>
>Communicate the beneficial outcomes of extreme change to others.
>
>Assume creative ownership over your life.
>
>Have no regrets about moving through this change.

Pioneer Preferred Environments:

Consider career experiences where:

The situation will soon significantly change.

Short term, high energy efforts, and complete turnarounds are the norm.

Great risk, also great rewards exist.

Complete transitions or conversions are taking place.

You would not benefit in environments where:

Both personally and professionally nothing ever changes.

You are relegated to performing the exact requirements of your previous job.

You perform without future career vision or direction.

You are trapped in a lifestyle/work style suffocating to you.

In review—

The Pioneer is a creative position enacting major changes in one's life. The demands of this position suggest that you accept the necessity to take great risks and grow accustomed to surviving the *rough waters* of unexpected events. As the Modifier position requires you to critique and redirect your job efforts, the Pioneer requires proficiency at creating an entirely new landscape of work and life. As you initially define the potential environments (both personal and professional) that appear to align most with your future needs, commit your actions entirely to the task of embracing the discovery of these new environments. You are transformed through personal and professional regeneration. Letting go of the old, identifying new *ports*, and re-hanging the *sails* are the themes of the Pioneer position. Learn to lift your foot gently off the shore as you push the new ship into the water.

Are you The Pioneer?

Discovering a totally new personal/professional life is important to you. Whole-life regeneration, retirement to new work, and defining oneself through whole-life transcendence are critical themes.

Career Transition: In Review

Career Transition, as found on the Career Lifecycle, is comprised of three positions, each in their own way preparing you to better handle the major changes in your career and life. The last of the Career Lifecycle stages, Career Transition strives for a seamless alignment of your personal and professional requirements, inclusive of respectful work relationships, rewards gained through professional contribution, and a complete personal/professional renovation. If you were not successful in gaining the appropriate knowledge required to develop your career well, you may discover the obstacles encountered here are enough to sink your ship, albeit temporarily.

Career Transition Exercise # 4

Review your completed Career Positioner. Were you able to finish the entire list of questions in the Career Planning section? Each one of the questions relates to a corresponding position on the Career Lifecycle. You may wish to revisit the position(s) that posed the most difficult questions for you and review the information again.

OFF COURSE: #5

Change Master

Change is one of the most reliable processes in the world. Today it cycles faster than at any time in recorded history. You might think that all humans are equipped to handle change; however, the change dynamic of today, whether elective or not, creates great stress. Constant change found in our lifestyles and through our work contribute to the stress experienced in contemporary society.

Whenever you look at how change impacts your career, it always arrives with two distinct and different options. There is the change that is inflicted upon you without much notice (**reactive**) and the change that you generate (**proactive**) that comes from choice. Either way, not being able to cope creates a great deal of emotional and physical disruption.

One of the best skills that you can possess in your career toolkit is the ability to be resilient and positive through change. Resiliency, however, is a learned behavior. As such, you can better manage the extremes that come along with the change; mitigating the emotional responses to it by having sound strategies for coping.

Perhaps it would be helpful for you to take a look at the behavior dynamic behind change. Change is like a ladder. Each rung as you climb the "change ladder" symbolizes another hurdle within the change process. As you undergo any change process you will always begin on the bottom rung.

Whether the change is chosen or elective, the first of your responses to change is **Denial**. If the change is forced upon you, you may not want to believe that it is happening. This may also cause you to behave as if nothing really **is** happening.

If the change is elective, you may believe that you will be OK with it until the change begins to impact the habits within your life. Then, you may deny that you were ever really committed to the change in the first place.

Denial is the result of lack of real proof. Either, 1) you really do not have the proof anything is occurring; or, 2) feel that change is unnecessary as responsibilities behind it begin to sink in. It is irrelevant if the change is perceived as good or bad, the response to it begins the same. Look at Jan's example.

The **first** step on the change ladder is **Denial**.

> Jan opens her e-mail and reads that her employer is eliminating her position. She is stunned. She notes that the date of separation is thirty days away. Jan decides that she can handle this, so she resumes her work; business as usual.
>
> When the company insists that she work *non-paid* overtime to help transition her job to a new person in another state, she is as equally committed to her job as ever.
>
> The company hires an outplacement firm to assist her in creating her new resume and conducting a job search; however, due to the increased workload required to close out her position, she neglects this new career requirement; her **personal** career requirement.
>
> Jan is in Denial; her behavior, on *automatic*. The change is not yet real to her.
>
> When in Denial, we want "real proof."

The **second** step on the change ladder is **Doubt**.

> Through discussions with family, friends and people at work, the reality of losing her job seems unlikely. She begins to doubt that it will really happen. After all, she has done a great job, and the company is well-respected. They really don't need to relocate the jobs; wouldn't that be more expensive?

> When in Doubt, we are saying, "Yes...but."

The **third** step on the change ladder is **Debate**.

> "Why is this change occurring in the first place?" she questions. After all, she has done a great job. She is certain that once they recognize this, they will have to reconsider their decision.

> Jan begins to debate whether or not she could have done better, worked harder, longer. It does not matter if she believes in the change, she feels disloyal in moving on.

> When in Debate, we look for blame or accountability: "What if they did this? What if I did that?"

The **fourth** step on the change ladder is **Decision**.

> Does Jan want to play victim or does she wish to be proactive in her personal responsibility to the future of her own career? Her ultimate decision to *accept* the change depends on her ability to acknowledge that this really is happening; to get past the doubt, to stop the "what-ifs," and to choose actions that will serve her well.

The final step results in either **Default** or a commitment to new **Action**.

> Default sends Jan down the rungs of the change ladder, while Action progresses her in a new and positive direction; one that is right for her!

This change model would work in similar fashion if Jan chose to leave her position. This is how it would unfold.

Denial

> Jan considers leaving her position because the company revenues have been declining. Fearful of a downsizing, she elects to consider other options. During her first week of preparing for her new job search, however, she is confronted with the enormous amount of work involved in updating her resume. She is in denial that her new job search is *really* even necessary.

Doubt

> Jan questions whether this is the best time to leave her employer; she might get a nice severance package if she decides to stay.

Debate

> It may be worth it to stay if the company would just do things *her* way. The debate continues as she weighs the pros and cons of staying.

Decision

> Jan begins to share her options with others. Of course, everyone has their own bias; she realizes that she needs to make the decision on her own.

> As she reaches the Decision point, Jan is faced with the ultimate choice, and with one foot on the shore and the other on the dock, she has to take the risk that her company may discover that she is seeking new work.

Action

> Jan commits, choosing to actively look for new employment. Although she has made the commitment, at some future point she may become discouraged. This discouragement may cause her to "climb" the change ladder anew.

How can you learn to be resilient through change? Here are some strategies:

- Know what you want.
- Go through change with a support system; tap into positive re-enforcements when you need them.
- Focus on positive expectations and outcomes; be realistic and concrete in what you want to have happen.
- Respect yourself, your skills and workplace potential.
- Leave doubt, fear and hesitation behind.
- Establish new boundaries for your new relationships.
- Consent to compromises; put overly high and unrealistic expectations into perspective.

As you strive to become a true Change Master, realize that it takes time, practice and perseverance. Being self-aware as you move up the change ladder will assist you in identifying any negative habits you may develop along the way.

Individual Change Model

Default (old)   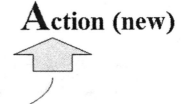 **A**ction (new)

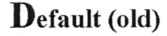

#4 Decide: I accept or do not accept the change

#3 Debate: I will need to adjust to the change

#2 Doubt: the change may not REALLY need to occur

#1 Denial: the change is not coming

EPILOGUE

It has been quite an adventure using the **CoachCompass®** to navigate through your Career Lifecycle. In summary, here are the positions presented again. Remember, it is likely that you will progress from the first position through the sixth position (in their stated order) early in your life. As your career matures, you will cross over into the Career Management or Career Transition stages. If you are feeling successful, then clearly you are able to apply the skills required for success in the position that you presently occupy. If you are feeling stuck or unhappy, it is time to review the requirements of that position, using some of the strategies listed, in order to gain the competency required to move past the obstacle.

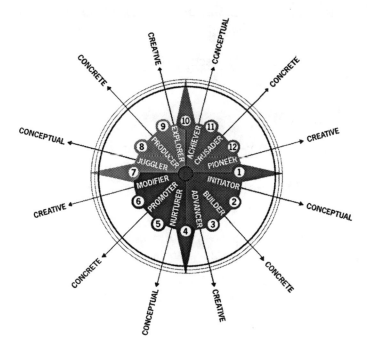

Career Planning:
Who I Am, What I Do, What I Want

Initiator (position #1)

You enter a career path (initiate) as soon as you become conscious of the things in your world most compelling to you. As you are introduced to basic experiences, you begin to see which of these you prefer. You are defining yourself through your authentic identity.

Whenever in your career you need to define who you are, exclusive from others, you are in the Initiator position.

Builder (position #2)

As you continue to build your skills and further engage in new activities, you also begin to determine which of these activities result in reliable and successful outcomes. You are building your vocational and life skills to your strengths.

Whenever you are focused *exclusively* on building skills or enhancing talents, you are in the Builder position.

Advancer (position #3)

As you continue in education, you have exposure to a variety of life and work experiences, defining those you enjoy. You are determining your preferences for an ideal career direction.

Whenever you are choosing among a variety of experiences to create a more focused career plan, you are in the Advancer position.

Obstacles to Effective Career Planning

Peer, parental and workplace expectations may interfere with your career planning. Knowing the trends of the time regarding vocational and educational options can assist you in further defining an appropriate career path—one that also increases your commitment to work through any obstacles.

Career Development: What I Represent, What I Promote, What I Evaluate

Nurturer (position #4)

As you begin to position yourself in school, vocational or work environments, you begin to establish a professional image. You are defining yourself through a membership role that will evolve over time as the needs of your career and your life evolve.

Whenever your professional image needs defining or redefining, you are in the Nurturer position.

Promoter (position #5)

Within the marketplace of work, you employ skills of persuasion and influence for the purpose of progressing to new jobs or new levels. You are promoting your professional value.

Whenever you are focused on getting ahead and require tools to market your true value, you are in the Promoter position.

Modifier (position #6)

At a career juncture, you will determine the necessary actions or adjustments that you must make to enhance or improve your circumstance. You are evaluating the requirements and conditions of your job.

Whenever you are making improvements to your job situation, you are in the Modifier position.

Obstacles to Effective Career Development

Complacency may interfere with your success. The continual process of establishing, progressing and re-evaluating is encouraged to continually optimize conditions of employment. The myth of the "steady" job causes the most risk.

Career Management: How I Integrate, How I Succeed, How I Investigate

Juggler (position #7)

Events such as marriage, a new family or other changes in your personal life cause stress and disharmony as you attempt to regain or restore whole-life equilibrium. You are defining the new priorities within your new work/life role.

The opposite position, the Initiator, represented personal preferences. With the Juggler, you are prioritizing your whole-life preferences; setting boundaries.

Whenever you are faced with a change in your personal life that creates stress in your career, you are in the Juggler position.

Producer (position #8)

Reaching career heights requires tapping into accumulative personal and professional resources. The opposite position, the Builder, introduced your talents. Now you are using those talents to claim success!

Whenever you access resources and commit to reaching the greatest destination of your career, you are in the Producer position.

Explorer (position #9)

Work motivations are under scrutiny; your job, no longer a good match. The opposite position, the Advancer, puts you on the path of experiential discovery, identifying environments that would offer you the best career fit. Now, you are on the path of motivational discovery, examining your greatest potential found through work.

Whenever you desire to explore your purpose for work, you are in the Explorer position.

Obstacles to Effective Career Management

The management of your career revolves around your ability to identify and revisit the values, systems and principles that you have created in your work and life. You are forced to look at your priorities, performance and the motivations affecting your career and life in a completely new way.

Career Transition: How I Achieve, How I Impact, How I Reinvent

Achiever (position #10)

Your career becomes upwardly mobile or results in job loss. The opposite position, the Nurturer, perpetuates a membership role within a network or team. The Achiever expands that role, sustaining self-respect and respect of others throughout all hierarchical changes.

Whenever you undertake any major status changes in your career, you are in the Achiever position.

Crusader (position #11)

Trends create shifts in the work environment; these changes impact the measurable value of your work effort. The opposite position, the Promoter, got you noticed for your workplace value. In the Crusader position, you are demanding that your professional value be adequately rewarded in kind.

Whenever you desire to be appropriately compensated or rewarded through your work, you are in the Crusader position.

Pioneer (position #12)

Life as you know it has just completed a major cycle. The opposite position, the Modifier, recommended evaluating your job; this position suggests redefining your entire life. You are revisiting and revising the requirements and conditions of your whole career/life.

Whenever the natural career/life expires (as in traditional retirement of the job), no longer meeting pre-established whole career/life requirements, you are in the Pioneer position.

Obstacles to Effective Career Transition

> Resisting the conditions and requirements demanded of change will result in great personal and professional liability. Change insists on the adaptation of new skills and behaviors. The natural state of career evolution requires you to live fully in the present, with a clear understanding that the career/life circumstances of the past will not return.

You have reached the end of your career journey. Visit the Appendix for additional Navigation Tools. You may wish to scan the worksheets to a copier and increase their size for optimal workability.

Bon Voyage!

APPENDIX

More Navigation Tools for Your Career

CAREER SUCCESS CHECK-UP

Review the following; can you answer **yes** to each question?

Define you: Who are you?
1. Does your career reflect your personal preferences?
2. Do you have a defined or established role-image or professional reputation?
3. Have you established and managed your priorities well at home and in work?
4. Do you rely on self-respect rather than career *symbols* to represent your professional reputation or achievement?

This first grouping considers your self-esteem, self-image, personal/professional boundaries and self-respect. The way that you perceive and treat yourself influences how others perceive and treat you. You will find success by defining and articulating your preferences.

Assess you: What do you do?
1. Could you describe your talents?
2. Is your career inventory marketable?
3. Have you kept an ongoing running inventory of accomplishments/resources?
4. Do you know what your contribution in the workplace is worth?

This second grouping considers your value to the world as measured by the level of your investment in your work. There is a direct correlation between your ability to recognize your accomplishments and the ability for employers to recognize workplace value. You will find success by defining and validating your talents.

Validate you: What do you want?

1. Have you explored a variety of career interests or paths?
2. Can you redirect your career at any time to better meet your requirements/needs?
3. Is your career action in alignment with your motivations or personal purpose?
4. If the circumstances of your career or life were to drastically change, are you prepared to identify the next conditions of your employment?

This final grouping deals with a direct alignment of your desires as they meet with your career/life expectations. Your willingness to discover, take risks and adapt to new things as your career and life change will reward you well! You will find success when you finally realize what you really want!

How did you do?

INDEPENDENT CHOICE ASSESSMENT: *The Initiator*

Are your choices based upon…?

Dependent Thinking

- A limited scope of perception
- An expression or wish to be cared for
- Reliance on others to drive choices, options
- Restrictions either self-imposed or imposed by others' directions
- Governed by higher authority
- The traditional work ethic
- The appropriate choice

Independent Thinking

- Personal self-esteem, personal belief of open-ended options
- Self-reliance
- Unrestricted thoughts, independent thoughts
- Willingness to take risks
- Innate desire to succeed
- Need to be competitive or creative
- A potential choice

It is imperative to feel personally empowered and to be able to make independent choices in your career.

THE LIKE-DO WELL MATRIX: *The Builder*

List below your likes and dislikes regarding vocational interests and activities. Your list in the first box and third box reflects the areas in which you should develop and learn. The shadowed box you should not bother to consider for educational or experiential pursuits. Use the following table to assist you in further defining these preferences.

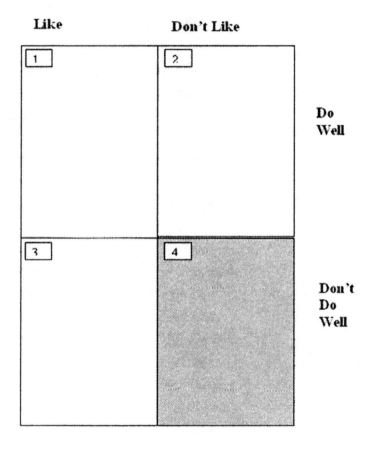

Like   Don't Like

1

2   Do Well

3

4   Don't Do Well

YOUR PREFERRED SKILLS: *The Builder*

Circle the top twelve skills you prefer to use and perform well. Write in any additional skills not listed.

analyze	meet deadlines	administer
audit	problem-solve	articulate
budget	speak publicly	confront
calculate	supervise	counsel
compute	schedule	demonstrate
review	plan	purvey
classify	conduct	arrange
compare	instruct	coach
compile	persuade	interview
count	present	listen
evaluate	identify	mentor
investigate	train	trust
locate	negotiate	articulate
manage	organize	perform
record	categorize	correspond
research	compose	create
synthesize	associate	design
arrange	mitigate	devise
compete	build	develop
decide	modify	assess
delegate	repair	edit
direct	drive	invent
explain	operate	research
teach	observe	resource
influence	inspect	solve

mediate	facilitate	compute
delegate	document	layout
maintain	innovate	implement
expedite	critique	attend
coordinate	assemble	resolve

These top twelve skills should be the ones that you enjoy using in your daily job.

PERSONAL INTERESTS: *The Advancer*

The following is a list of characteristics, preferences and interests. Go through the list. The first eight are career interests, the last six are job interests. For each characteristic rate how important it is for you to have that characteristic in your career or job. Use the following scale:

1. Very important
2. Somewhat important
3. Not very important
4. Not important at all

_____   1. Help Others

_____   2. Contact with Others

_____   3. Work with Others

_____   4. Work Alone

_____   5. Lead Others

_____   6. Learn New Things

_____   7. Career Security

_____   8. Create/Innovate

_____   9. Economic Reward

_____   10. Variety, Excitement, or Adventure

_____   11. Fast Pace or Pressure

_____   12. Consistency and Predictability

_____   13. Independence and Freedom

_____   14. Measure Performance

List the three lowest scores below. These are the things you consider when choosing career interests and workplace options.

Top Three: _____ _____ _____

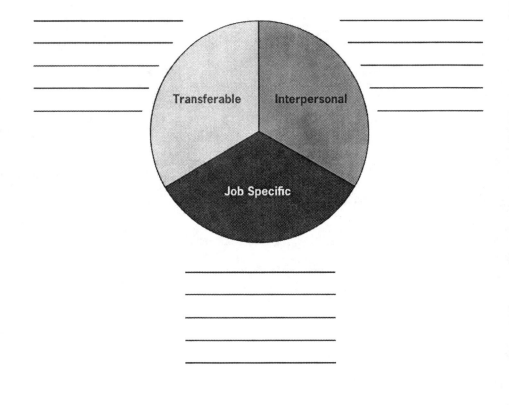

PARTNERING/TEAMWORK ASSESSMENT: *The Nurturer*

Consider the statements below as they relate to you within the workplace. Your answers will define the role you would prefer to "play" in the workplace. Place a check next to the ones that most describe you.

1. I tend to be a team player.

2. I like to work alone.

3. I assume a "shared understanding" exists when we are trying to achieve a goal.

4. I appreciate thorough communication and procedures in the planning and implementation of my work.

5. I collaborate with others regarding the work and then go about my individual task to contribute.

6. I know my job and perform it.

7. I constantly thrive on challenge, enjoy stretching my skills.

8. I like rules, structure and guidelines.

9. I like knowing and trusting my skills and instincts to do the job under stress.

10. I enjoy a long problem-solving process rather than a quick fix.

11. I make quick decisions that serve everyone.

12. I prefer a steady, reliable day without many surprises.

13. I adjust my actions to meet the needs of the team or environment.

14. I rely on existing habits that have served me in the past.

If you chose more even than odd statements, you may find it difficult to succeed as the workplace evolves and your role changes. These changes may require you to augment your actions or habits if you are seeking to sustain effectiveness in a new role. One of the best skills to learn is that of Networking.

MARKETABLE SKILLS ASSESSMENT: *The Promoter*

Review and assess the following skills areas that permit you to positively and effectively promote your career value. Score each area on a scale of 1-3, with 1 being most effective and 3 being least effective to determine your most Marketable areas.

Basic Skills

_ Written/Verbal Communication

_ E-communication

_ Simple Mathematical

Personal Skills

_ Positive Attitude

_ Value System

_ Accountability, Responsibility

_ Decision-making

_ Positive Self-concept

_ Sense of Competence

_ Competitive Spirit

Job Attainment Skills

_ Network

_ Industry Awareness

_ Resume

_ Interview Skill

_ Job Search Etiquette

_ Portfolio Development

_ "The Toot" (can genuinely articulate benefit to others)

Job Survival Skills
- _ Workplace Maturity
- _ Professional Appropriateness
- _ Employer Evolution
- _ Job Mastery
- _ Positive Human Relations
- _ Partnering Philosophy

Career Development Skills
- _ Assess Preferences, Skills, Interests
- _ Establish Work Role and Relate Aptitudes to Multiple Areas
- _ Promote Value with Career Marketplace
- _ Assess and Redirect Career, GAP Aware

Professional Development Skills
- _ Self-directed
- _ Continuous learner
- _ Trendsetter
- _ Mentor
- _ Leader
- _ Others_____

JOB/CAREER EVALUATION: *The Modifier*

Place a check in either the left or right column on each line of each page. Total the number of checks within each column at the bottom. If your right column total is substantially higher than your left column total, you need to seriously redirect your career path.

YOUR JOB/YOUR CAREER

___You are marketable to other businesses	___ You are locked into your job
___Your workdays go quickly	___ Your workdays drag on
___You are in charge of your career	___ You feel overworked, undervalued, trapped
___You are willing to work for career success	___ You prefer not to think about your career
___You are satisfied with your compensation	___ Your compensation is limited
___You have a sense of humor about work	___ You think about your work and get angry
___You enjoy your daily tasks	___ You dislike the tasks that you perform
___You are constantly learning new things	___ You are bored, do the job in your sleep
___Your job holds your interest	___ Your job is just a job
___Your responsibilities make sense to you	___ You are tired of doing things w/o purpose
Total	Total

YOUR ENVIRONMENT/INDUSTRY

____You get along with your supervisor	____ Seeing your supervisor fills you with dread
____You are included in decisions	____ You get orders, not direction or support
____You are recognized for your performance	____ You are never rewarded for a good job
____You enjoy your work	____ You are resentful about work
____You are accountable for your performance	____ You are overlooked for promotion
____You are relaxed with your boss/coworkers	____ Your boss/ peers/subordinates think you are incompetent
____Your salary/compensation is competitive	____ Your compensation is capped.
____Your organization is healthy	____ Your organization is making you sick
____You might enjoy your supervisor's job	____ You would hate your supervisor's job
____You have been given adequate tools to perform the task at hand	____ You are overworked, begging for resources
____You are proud of the work that you are in	____ You lie about the work/job you do
____Your organization appreciates and rewards its employees	____ Your organization's turnover is high
Total	Total

Do you have a higher score in the right column? If so, consider why these conditions exist and how you could possibly change them.

EQUILIBRIUM PLAN FOR HOME AND WORK:
The Juggler

List all of the activities that primarily make up your day in the left column. Define their priority and the time that you spend with them. Review the tasks to see if the priority is low; see if this item can be delegated. Eliminate both those low in priority, as well as those that take the most time.

Activity or Task (✓ if possible to delegate)	Priority (high/low)	Time Spent
_____	_____	_____
_____	_____	_____
_____	_____	_____
_____	_____	_____
_____	_____	_____
_____	_____	_____
_____	_____	_____
_____	_____	_____
_____	_____	_____
_____	_____	_____
_____	_____	_____
_____	_____	_____
_____	_____	_____

PROJECT PLAN: *The Producer*

Complete the following success plan. Are you able to access and assemble the resources that you will need?

What resources do I need? (people, data, functions)

When is my success date? (when does this become an accomplishment)

What standards will I set for a quality outcome? (ethics, reputation)

What will allow me to confirm quality benchmarks at every stage of the project?

What will I do to maximize efficiency? (timelines, work/life balance)

What will I do when obstacles arise? (solicit assistance from others, learn something new)

What alternatives will I consider if my success is dependent upon others? (Plan B or C)

What will determine my final success?

Write an accomplishment statement describing in detail what I will be able to measure as a result of a successful outcome.

MOTIVATIONAL SURVEY: *The Explorer*

Preview the entire list. Check the items that mean the most to you and drive you to action. X the items that mean the least. Then prioritize the ones that mean the most. These are the things that align with your chosen purpose in work; if given importance these will permit full realization of your potential.

- Achievement (status, persistence)
- Aesthetics (environmental enjoyment, appreciation of beauty/ art or culture)
- Altruism (regard or devotion to service, supporting the interests of others)
- Autonomy (self-directed and self-determined, making independent choices)
- Creativity (innovative, experiential)
- Emotionally Secure (healthy ego, inner peace, recognize/cope with inner conflicts)
- Family (parents, children, spouse)
- Health (sound in body, sound in mind)
- Honesty (frank, genuine, authentic)
- Justice (fair, impartial, allied with truth)
- Knowledge (learning, curiosity, wisdom)
- Love (warmth, caring, devotion)
- Loyalty (allegiance to a person, group or dogma)
- Morality (ethical, personal honor, integrity)
- Physical Appearance (concern for attractiveness or personal presentation)
- Pleasure (satisfaction, joy, gratification)
- Power (control, authority, influence or persuasion over others)
- Recognition (valued, accepted, respected)

- Faith (relationship to higher being, spirituality)
- Skill (application of your knowledge, talents, effective use of talents)
- Wealth (possessions, acquisitions, riches)
- Wisdom (mature insight, intuition, knowing)

List your top three: 1.   2.   3.

List your least three: 1.   2.   3.

The motivations listed above are positive motivations; however, you may find that you chose the negative motivations when it comes to your career. These include fear, worry, shame and inadequacy.

Do you have the courage to perform your work according to your purpose?

ACHIEVEMENT ASSESSMENT: *The Achiever*

Circle the number of each statement that is aligned with your intention. How prepared are you to achieve success in an uncertain workplace climate?

1. I desire to get ahead and will persevere to do so.

2. I invest time and energy in my professional achievement.

3. I take full responsibility for who I am and where I am in the career process.

4. I recognize my strengths and abilities and those that exist in others.

5. I am fully prepared to make adjustments to my current work identity to be successful in a new one.

6. I am willing to address or to confront circumstances that may be holding me back or preventing my achievement.

7. I am willing to work through any changes that affect my relationships (supervisors, peers and subordinates) within my work environment and my work community.

8. I clearly appreciate the achievements that I can claim and know that these achievements were accomplished through my hard work and with the contributions of others.

9. I believe that prior achievements do not ensure future successes.

10. Changes in employment status potentially offer new and interesting opportunities for achievement in other areas or other careers.

11. I measure my value and achievement through my own eyes.

12. I have a healthy relationship with the symbols of success (money, possessions, etc.)

13. I have over the years been successful at adapting my sense of self and my needs to the circumstance in which I find myself.

14. I have a respect for my own position within my career and respect others in kind.

15. I work a reasonable and level schedule without placing undue strain on myself or those around me.

16. I am of value to myself and to others regardless of the position I hold or my place within the work hierarchy.

If you can answer "yes" to all of these statements, then you are prepared to weather the storms of uncertainty as your career grows and changes. Which statements gave you the most difficulty?

EQUITY WITHIN WORK: *The Crusader*

In each case, choose which of the paired statements that best reflects your agreement.

1. *My contribution at work is rewarded in kind in terms of money, satisfaction and benefits.*
2. My contribution at work is not rewarded fairly in terms of money, job satisfaction and benefits.

3. *Because of changes in the workplace, I am able to better contribute to the overall goals of the organization.*
4. Because of the changes in the workplace, I am restricted from contributing, as I once did, to the goals of the organization.

5. *I constantly see possibilities for improvement and have the ability to make suggestions.*
6. I constantly see possibilities for improvement but have no venue through which to make suggestions.

7. *The work that I presently do is very satisfying and reminds me that I bring value to the organization.*
8. The work that I do is not satisfying and reminds me that I would rather spend time in another environment where my contributions would be valued.

9. *I receive regular and positive feedback or direction regarding the work that I do.*
10. I hardly ever or never receive positive feedback or direction regarding the work that I do.

11. *I am rewarded in kind for my contributions.*
12. I feel that I am just making what is needed to get by.

13. *I have always felt comfortable when negotiating for money, time off or other personal benefits in my job.*
14. I have never felt comfortable asking for what I am worth or getting special privileges.

Total: Odd_____

Total: Even_____

If your scores reflect more even than odd, review "Off Course: Equity."

REINVENTING WORK AND LIFE: *The Pioneer*

Below is a short checklist for complete career/life transformation. Complete each assignment before you decide to take the leap.

- o   Identify and accept the reasons for this change.

- o   Survey the new landscape for work and living.

- o   Identify finances and funding required for the change.

- o   Create a new career direction or at least a sound idea for one.

- o   Identify your new life model and how it will fit with the new career.

- o   Identify a new network or supports to assist you through the change.

- o   Identify new skills areas or new education that you may be required to complete.

- o   Discuss the impact of the change with friends and family members.

- o   Meet with accountants, attorneys or insurance agents regarding the changes.

- o   Create new communication tools that will promote your new choice.

- o   Set a target date.

- o   Establish an exit strategy.

- o   Establish an entrance strategy.

CONDITIONS AND REQUIREMENTS: *The Pioneer*

List below your present life and work conditions. These are things such as: you live in a big house, you drive an expensive car, or you like to travel. List your career and life requirements, both acceptable and not, that you need to perform in order to meet your life conditions. Box one will illustrate what you prefer next in both your personal life and your work obligation required by it. The last shaded box contains those conditions and requirements that are no longer acceptable in your life.

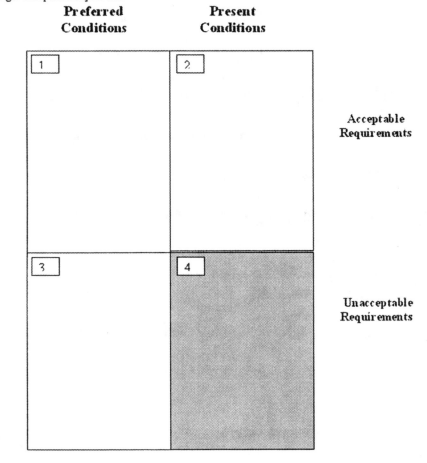

Preferred Conditions   **Present Conditions**

1

2

Acceptable Requirements

3

4

Unacceptable Requirements

THE CAREER COACH POSITIONER

By answering the questions below, you will be able to identify the best starting point for your career development and career management efforts. If you have difficulty answering any of these questions, consider the respective number; each relates to the 12 Positions of the Career Lifecycle.

1. Who are you? (define yourself)

2. What do you do? What do you presently possess in terms of skills, abilities, talents that could be applied in a job or vocation?

3. What do you want from your career? What do you consider to be your primary career direction or path?

4. What role do you play in your career? How do you establish and maintain your memberships, affiliations and your relationships within the workplace?

5. How do you promote yourself? How do you present your value?

6. What career options are available to you? How would you evaluate them?

7. What are your personal values? How do you determine your priorities with your family and work?

8. What success assets do you possess? How do you tap the resources needed to ensure your success?

9. What are your motivations for work? How do you define purpose in what you do?

10. How do you measure your achievements? Have your career relationships changed?

11. How are you valued/rewarded through your work? Does your contribution impact your work environment and reward you in return?

12. If you were to do anything in the world, including change your career and life completely, what would it look like? What in your life would drastically change?

Suggested Online Assessments for Each Position

Conceptual: (Initiator, Nurturer, Juggler, and Achiever)

Conceptual positions refer to the roles identified throughout the entire career/life dynamic.

> **Initiator**
> Keirsey Temperament Sorter
> www.keirsey.com
>
> True Colors
> www.mytruecolors.com
>
> **Nurturer**
> DISC Personal Profile
> www.discprofile.com
>
> Enneagram
> www.similarminds.com
>
> **Juggler**
> Life Balance Guide
> www.albertadoctors.org/bcm/ama/ama-
> website.nsf/AllDoc/87256DB000705C3F87256E0500552933/
> $File/life_balance_assessment. PDF
>
> **Achiever**
> Managing People Quiz
> www.smallbiz.nsw.gov.au/textonly/resources/tools/quizzes/
> ManagingPeople.html
>
> Leadership Self-Assessment
> http://www.ainc-inac.gc.ca/pr/pub/selfas_e.pdf

As all Conceptual positions rely on roles we play in our career life, here is an additional fun site of interest to assist you in identifying your role as you were in the "olden days."

http://www.cmi-lmi.com/kingdomality.html

Concrete: (Builder, Promoter, Producer, Crusader)

Concrete positions refer to the personal and professional value measured within the workplace.

Builder
Who are you vocationally?
www.cmi-lmi.com/kingdomality.html

IQ Test
http://www.iqtest.com/

Promoter
Successful Marketing
www.smallbiz.nsw.gov.au/textonly/resources/tools/quizzes/
SuccessfulMarketing.html

Marketing Quiz (when you take it, relate it to yourself as "a company of one").
http://www.marketingprofs.com/Quiz/quizindex.asp

Producer
Entrepreneur Quiz
www.wd.gc.ca/apps/amianent.nsf

Success Quiz (what does it mean to you?)
http://www.startupbiz.com/Success/Success_Quiz.htm

Crusader
Altruistic Quiz
www.usnews.com/usnews/doubleissue/heroes/quiz.htm

Are You Happy Quiz
http://www.oprah.com/spiritself/omag/
ss_omag_200403_happyquiz.jhtml

As all Concrete positions rely on some kind of success measurement, here is an additional site of interest to assist you in identifying your salary value appropriate to your skills.

www.salary.com

Creative: (Advancer, Modifier, Explorer, Pioneer)

Creative positions refer to choices; the decisions and discoveries of our career and life.

Advancer
Career Exploration Inventory
www.jist.com

Career Search Quiz
http://www.career.uno.edu/pdfs/Career%20Search%20Quiz.pdf

Modifier
Career Change
www.quintcareers.com/career_change_quiz.html

Flying Solo
http://www.flyingsolo.com.au/suitedsolo.htm

Explorer
Motivation Quiz
www.snc.edu/socsci/chair/333/motvquiz.htm

MAPP
www.assessment.com

Pioneer
Change Quiz
www.kiplinger.com/tools/careerchange.php

Are You Ready to Retire Quiz
http://www.asec.org/rrr.htm

As all Creative positions consider choices and change, here is an additional site of interest to assist you in coping with changes, both major and minor.

Resiliency Quiz
http://www.resiliency.com/htm/resiliencyquiz.htm

Disclaimer: Please note that this list does not imply a direct recommendation or endorsement of these exact assessment products, but simply refers to them as suggested venues for these modes. As the Internet is a dynamic and changing tool, note that these URL addresses may undergo changes in both venue and cost as this book remains on the shelf.

ABOUT THE AUTHORS

WENDY B. ADAMS, B.S., CCM, GCDF

Wendy has assisted thousands of professionals and numerous businesses through workforce transitions over the last two decades. Her clients have included executives, government organizations and Fortune 100 businesses. She has provided coaching, consulting and training to individuals, groups and organizations in all areas of Career Planning, Development, Management and Transition working within the complete lifecycle of workforce development and training; Recruitment through Retention.

Wendy has developed and delivered over 400 training programs including her favorite, **The Business of Career Coaching**, and was the first professional to present Internet training for both job seekers and employers in the State of Maryland. A columnist in print media and e-zines, she continues to share her knowledge of the ever-changing workplace.

She has held membership in the Mid-Atlantic Career and Life Planning Network, the International Coach Federation, the International Association of Career Management Professionals (ACP), the Career Masters Institute and is a prior Board Member of the American Society of Training and Development.

As the Founder and Managing Partner of *The Career Coach, CCC*, a performance management and career services company serving professionals within all workforce environments, she is the creator of the **CoachCompass®**: System for Coaching and HR Professionals. As the primary author of this book, she brings her vision, talent and energy together to ensure that career success is possible for everyone.

GENE A. POMETTO, JR., M.A., M.P.H., LCPC, NBCCH

As an original pioneer in the holistic health community, Gene has devoted the last two decades of his career to the professional areas of organizational development and training. Recognized as a performance-driven and quality-oriented professional, his educational credentials in Public Health (Johns Hopkins University), Applied Behavioral Sciences (Johns Hopkins University) and Humanistic Psychology (State University of West Georgia), coupled with a clinical license in professional counseling and a national certification in clinical hypnotherapy, complement his innate talent to effectively coach, motivate and guide clients to the successful achievement of their personal, career or organizational goals.

Gene has held membership in the Association of Humanistic Psychology, the American Public Health Association, the American Society of Training and Development, the American Mental Health Counselors Association and the American Counselors Association. Serving as the Senior Partner of *The Career Coach. CCC*, he is a valued contributor to the refinement and usability of the **CoachCompass**® System for individuals wishing a more successful and satisfying career life. Gene is accommo-dating its use for counseling professionals desiring to provide more consistent and valuable life services to their clients.

Partners in life and work, Wendy and Gene can be reached through their company website, *The Career Coach. CCC*, at www.coachcompass.com.

INDEX

175

978-0-595-34528-1
0-595-34528-X

Printed in the United States
61825LVS00005B/103-129